P9-BYD-941

# Jossey-Bass Teacher

Jossey-Bass Teacher provides educators with practical knowledge and tools to create a positive and lifelong impact on student learning. We offer classroom-tested and research-based teaching resources for a variety of grade levels and subject areas. Whether you are an aspiring, new, or veteran teacher, we want to help you make every teaching day your best.

From ready-to-use classroom activities to the latest teaching framework, our value-packed books provide insightful, practical, and comprehensive materials on the topics that matter most to K–12 teachers. We hope to become your trusted source for the best ideas from the most experienced and respected experts in the field.

# Differentiated Instruction Made Easy

Hundreds of Multi-Level Activities for All Learners (Grades 2–8)

Phyllis Kaplan
Virginia Rogers
Rande Webster

JOSSEY-BASS
A Wiley Imprint
www.josseybass.com

Copyright © 2008 by John Wiley & Sons, Inc. All rights reserved.

Published by Jossey-Bass
A Wiley Imprint
989 Market Street, San Francisco, CA 94103-1741—www.josseybass.com

No part of this publication may be reproduced, stored in a retrieval system, or transmitted in any form or by any means, electronic, mechanical, photocopying, recording, scanning, or otherwise, except as permitted under Section 107 or 108 of the 1976 United States Copyright Act, without either the prior written permission of the publisher, or authorization through payment of the appropriate per-copy fee to the Copyright Clearance Center, Inc., 222 Rosewood Drive, Danvers, MA 01923, 978-750-8400, fax 978-646-8600, or on the Web at www.copyright.com. Requests to the publisher for permission should be addressed to the Permissions Department, John Wiley & Sons, Inc., 111 River Street, Hoboken, NJ 07030, 201-748-6011, fax 201-748-6008, or online at www.wiley.com/go/permissions.

Permission is given for individual classroom teachers to reproduce the pages and illustrations for classroom use. Reproduction of these materials for an entire school system is strictly forbidden.

Readers should be aware that Internet Web sites offered as citations and/or sources for further information may have changed or disappeared between the time this was written and when it is read.

Limit of Liability/Disclaimer of Warranty: While the publisher and author have used their best efforts in preparing this book, they make no representations or warranties with respect to the accuracy or completeness of the contents of this book and specifically disclaim any implied warranties of merchantability or fitness for a particular purpose. No warranty may be created or extended by sales representatives or written sales materials. The advice and strategies contained herein may not be suitable for your situation. You should consult with a professional where appropriate. Neither the publisher nor author shall be liable for any loss of profit or any other commercial damages, including but not limited to special, incidental, consequential, or other damages.

Jossey-Bass books and products are available through most bookstores. To contact Jossey-Bass directly call our Customer Care Department within the U.S. at 800-956-7739, outside the U.S. at 317-572-3986, or fax 317-572-4002.

Jossey-Bass also publishes its books in a variety of electronic formats. Some content that appears in print may not be available in electronic books.

ISBN: 978-0-4703-7235-7

Printed in the United States of America
FIRST EDITION
*PB Printing*      10  9  8  7  6  5  4  3  2  1

# About This Book

The students sitting in our classrooms represent a rainbow of hopeful learners with diverse backgrounds and abilities. This book provides teachers with an opportunity to look at learning for these students in a different way. There are no limits to the curricular strategies and learning tools that a creative teacher can provide to students, each of whom has gifts and challenges. The concepts in this book are built on a foundation of multilevel (learning levels from basic to advanced) and multimodality (based on learning styles, multiple intelligence theory, and other ways of matching learning to learners) activities and skill builders.

Classroom teachers are faced with too many repetitive and rote drills and lessons that do not enhance the relationships between teachers and students or between students and successful learning experiences. It is our hope that this book will encourage teachers and students to design their own learning games, contracts, activities, and tools to encourage unusual topics that reflect individual passions. Teaching to students' passions may be the beginning step in developing students who are finally motivated to learn.

# Introduction

Increasing numbers of students with diverse educational needs are filling American classrooms across the nation. English language learners and students with special education needs compose the largest groups of diverse learners in today's classrooms. Diverse students create new and different challenges within the teaching profession, especially in the areas of instruction, curriculum, and assessment. Scholars and educators concerned with the educational challenges of these diverse student groups have urged teachers to consider the unique learning characteristics and learning styles of their students when planning education programs.

*Response to intervention, individualized instruction, direct instruction, multiple intelligence theory, differentiated instruction,* and *universal design* are some of the terms used to describe types of pedagogy developed in response to the call for instruction designed to meet the needs of each student. This pedagogy is characterized by curricula that are organized around powerful, creative ideas; interactive teaching strategies; active student involvement; and personal, social, and community activities. There are, however, few practical, activity-based books that address the ways in which teachers can use these strategies to meet the unique curricular needs of each student in their classrooms.

The purpose of this book is to provide general and special education classroom teachers with multilevel activities for students in many subject areas. The book is not designed to teach basic concepts. The activities included in this volume have been created to provide interesting learning alternatives that reinforce and offer practice in previously taught basic concepts. This book will enable teachers to design learning opportunities that are motivating, offer adjustable levels of challenge, and provide students with curricular choices that encourage their involvement.

Teachers will find here hundreds of creative ideas that motivate and reinforce learning for all students in grades 2 to 8. The book is intended to supplement standards-based curricula by

- Providing materials that support standards and benchmarks
- Permitting students who function at different skill levels, including those with English language and special education needs, to participate in similar tasks
- Enabling all students to experience success with materials that reflect their learning preferences

- Allowing teachers to vary the requirements and expectations for learning and expressing knowledge, including the degree of difficulty and the means of evaluation
- Including open-ended materials that allow for the design of systematic learning experiences
- Offering creative worksheets, task cards, gameboards, task wheels, and other means for motivating and reinforcing learning
- Encouraging cooperation and respect among students with a wide range of individual differences
- Providing practice and reinforcement for sharing, creativity, self-motivation, and decision making
- Ensuring the participation of all students
- Encouraging students to select independent learning opportunities
- Providing valuable informal assessment information

Every student can achieve success when the teacher instructs and supports the students' ability to select from a variety of activities while systematically adding activities that enhance the learning process. Support for student choice is reflected in the student-teacher contracts found within each content area.

## Who This Book Is For

This book was designed for use with students who have a wide range of abilities and challenges. It can be used with students who have no "special needs," those who have learning challenges, those who have language differences, those who need that added spark to ignite their desire to learn new concepts—in other words, all students!

This book has also been created for educators who know that students need to learn about their strengths, challenges, passions, and caring for others, and about the importance of the personal choices that are part of becoming successful adults. Classroom teachers are increasingly burdened with daily expectations and requirements. This book provides options that will enable each teacher to present material as they choose in order to promote creativity and provide students with successful experiences. At the same time, these learning opportunities are aligned with state curriculum standards and benchmarks.

## The Components of This Book

This book contains learning strategies and tools for reading, math, science, written expression, and other areas related to the core curriculum. In addition, there are chapters on art, music, media, service learning, and peace. There are several components to the book that may be used across each of the subject-specific areas.

1. ***Contracts.*** These are part of each subject-area chapter. Each contract includes an agreement form that allows both the teacher and the student to choose specific activities. The student may have favorite activities, which usually match their learning strengths. The teacher has the opportunity to select additional activities to meet each individual learner's challenges and needs. Everyone wins. Each contract has dozens of activities to choose from. For many students, there may be too many options. Teachers are encouraged to reduce the number of activities per contract and add their own creative ideas.

2. ***Specific task cards and wheels.*** Many of the subject-area chapters contain wheels and task cards specific to the content area. The directions for the use of these items are straightforward and can be adapted to meet the needs of each learner.

3. ***Multilevel gameboards.*** These gameboards are open-ended and can be played by groups of students functioning at different academic levels (see each gameboard's instructions). While designing their own games, the students are also practicing life skills, such as sharing, taking turns, and fair play.

4. ***Spinners.*** These tools can be used with gameboards or on their own. They are open-ended and can serve to reinforce skills and abilities for individuals or groups of learners.

5. ***Open-ended add-ons.*** The final section contains graph paper, diary tablet sheets, and other tools that can be used with various activities.

# About the Authors

**Phyllis Kaplan, Ph.D.,** directs the Special Education Mild/Moderate Credential Program of the Educational Psychology Department at California State University, East Bay. For many years Dr. Kaplan taught students classified as learning disabled, severely multiply disabled, and others facing special challenges. A popular speaker and presenter, she consults with school districts and community education projects. Kaplan is Founder and Director of H.A.T.C.H. (Helping Another Toward Creative Happiness), a community-based project serving the disabled, their families, and involved others through a one-to-one companion/tutor effort.

**Virginia Rogers** is a semi-retired educator with more than 40 years of teaching experience in regular, special, and higher education. In addition to her years as an instructor, Rogers has also worked as a school psychologist, consultant, and Director of the Special Education Teaching Intern Program at California State University, East Bay.

**Rande Webster, Ed.D.,** is associate professor of Education and Director of Special Education Credential Programs at Dominican University of California, San Rafael. She writes and presents at regional and national conferences. Webster is the president-elect of the California Association of Professors in Special Education (CAPSE).

# Acknowledgments

For the children who taught us how to teach. A special thanks to Carolyn Shaw for keeping us organized.

# Sample Contract

## Phonics Tasks

Now that you are ready to work on phonics:

☐   1. Name _____ words that begin with _____.

☑   2. Make an \_\_\_\_alphabet\_\_\_\_ book. Use the following elements:

     ☐ Consonants _____     ☑ Blends \_\_\_\_cl\_\_\_\_

     ☐ Vowels _____        ☐ Digraphs _____

☐   3. Name _____ words that end with _____.

☑   4. Name \_\_\_\_8\_\_\_\_ words that have \_\_\_\_"am"\_\_\_\_ in the \_\_\_\_middle\_\_\_\_.

☐   5. List _____ words from the _____ family.

☑   6. Make up a \_\_\_\_poem\_\_\_\_ using \_\_\_\_10\_\_\_\_ words from the \_\_\_\_diagraph\_\_\_\_ family.

☐   7. Make a list of _____ words with the ☐ short ☐ long vowel _____.

☐   8. Find _____ pictures of things that have the ☐ short ☐ long vowel sound _____.

☐   9. Draw _____ pictures that have the same _____ sound as _____.

☐ 10. Make _____ flash cards of words that ☐ begin ☐ end with _____.

☐ 11. Create a card game with your flash cards.

# Contents

## Part 1 Specific Subject Area Activities    1

**Contents**

# Part 2 Gameboards, Wheels, Open-Ended Add-ons, and Awards  181

# Specific Subject Area Activities

# Reading Activities

Included in this chapter are activities designed to make reading more rewarding, more motivating, and simply more exciting! These activities are not meant to take the place of a good reading program but rather are intended to supplement such a program and support students' reading skills. They can be used to reinforce skills, to provide practice and repetition when necessary, and to enrich the curriculum.

The materials in this chapter lend themselves to various instructional methods, whether group or individual, student directed or teacher directed. Many of the activities can be used in learning or game centers, and many can be used in other curricular areas that involve the reading process.

The multilevel contracts, task cards, spinners, and worksheets offered in this chapter can be duplicated and used to support many of the skills necessary for reading. It is impossible, of course, to include all of the skills, but the materials can be used as beginning points for implementing your own ideas and to meet students' needs.

# New Word Treasure Chest Contract

I, _____, agree to

collect _____ new words for my New Word Treasure Chest, and I

will complete _____ tasks to help me add to my word collection.

## New Words

_____

_____

_____

_____

_____

_____

_____

_____

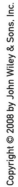
Copyright © 2008 by John Wiley & Sons. Inc.

**Differentiated Instruction Made Easy**

# New Word Treasure Chest: Getting Started

You will need a box and a set of blank word cards.

- ☐ 1. Get a box to use as your New Word Treasure Chest. The box should be big enough to hold three-by-five cards, but not too big.
- ☐ 2. Label the box with your name and a creative title.
- ☐ 3. Label each of twenty-six three-by-five cards with one letter of the alphabet.
- ☐ 4. File the lettered cards in your New Word Treasure Chest box in alphabetical order.
- ☐ 5. Use this box to store the word cards you will need for the following tasks.

Copyright © 2008 by John Wiley & Sons. Inc.

# New Word Treasure Chest: Tasks

Now that you have created your New Word Treasure Chest box:

☐  1. Write all of your new words, each on a separate card.

☐  2. Trace and say each word on your new word

cards _____ times.

☐  3. Copy _____ of your words on a piece of paper.

☐  4. Write or type your words without looking at the cards.

☐  5. Draw a picture on each of _____ word cards that describes the word.

☐  6. Use _____ of your words in sentences.
   ☐ Write ☐ Type ☐ Illustrate your sentences.

☐  7. Read _____ of your words to a friend.

☐  8. Make a dictionary in which you write the definitions of your new words.

☐  9. Use your word cards with a multilevel gameboard.

☐ 10. Write a ☐ poem ☐ story ☐ song ☐ letter ☐ other using

_____ of your new words.

☐ 11. Create a crossword puzzle using _____ of your new words.

☐ 12. Find _____ synonyms for _____ of your words.

☐ 13. Find _____ antonyms for _____ of your words.

☐ 14. Select _____ of your words. ☐ Add a prefix.
   ☐ Add a suffix.

☐ 15. Create as many little words as you can from _____ of your words.

Copyright © 2008 by John Wiley & Sons, Inc.

# Phonics Contract

I, _____, hereby agree to complete _____

phonics tasks by _____.

Date

I will choose _____ tasks myself and _____ will be assigned.

Write your sounds or words here:

_____

_____

_____

_____

_____

_____

_____

_____

_____

_____

_____


_____
Teacher


_____
Student

Copyright © 2008 by John Wiley & Sons, Inc.

# Phonics Tasks

Now that you are ready to work on phonics:

☐ 1. Name _____ words that begin with _____.

☐ 2. Make a _____ book. Use the following elements:

    ☐ Consonants _____   ☐ Blends _____

    ☐ Vowels _____   ☐ Digraphs _____

☐ 3. Name _____ words that end with _____.

☐ 4. Name _____ words that have _____ in

    the _____.

☐ 5. List _____ words from the _____ family.

☐ 6. Make up a _____ using _____ words from

    the _____ family.

☐ 7. Make a list of _____ words with the ☐ short ☐ long

    vowel _____.

☐ 8. Find _____ pictures of things that have the ☐ short

    ☐ long vowel sound _____.

☐ 9. Draw _____ pictures that have the same

    _____ sound as _____.

☐ 10. Make _____ flash cards of words that ☐ begin

    ☐ end with _____.

☐ 11. Create a card game with your flash cards.

Copyright © 2008 by John Wiley & Sons. Inc.

# Phonics Tasks *(continued)*

☐ 12. Use your flash cards to play ☐ a multilevel gameboard ☐ card game ☐ other.

☐ 13. Look in _____ and find _____ words that _____ with _____.

☐ 14. Make a phonics spinner with _____.

☐ 15. Use your phonics spinner to make _____ words.

☐ 16. Use your phonics spinner with a gameboard.

☐ 17. Find _____ words in your _____ that have _____ syllables.

☐ 18. Choose _____ words from your _____. Write them and tell how many syllables are in each.

☐ 19. Type on the computer _____ _____ words that have _____ sounds.

☐ 20. Write a _____ using _____ words that _____ with _____.

☐ 21. Create your own activity.

Copyright © 2008 by John Wiley & Sons, Inc.

# Phonics Task Cards

## Find the Rhymes

- ☐ Look up
- ☐ Write
- ☐ Tape
- ☐ Tell

all the words you can think of that rhyme with _____.

- Time yourself.
- Do it in _____ seconds.
- Have a friend time you for _____.

## How Does It End?

- ☐ Look up
- ☐ Write
- ☐ Tape
- ☐ Tell

words that have the _____ ending.

- Use each word in a sentence.
- Make a flash card for each word.
- Write each word _____ times.

## The Vowel Owl

- Find all the _____ letter words you can that the Vowel Owl is hiding.
- Let the Vowel Owl help you find

  _____ words in which the
  - ☐ consonant _____
  - ☐ short vowel _____
  - ☐ long vowel _____

  are checked.

## Graph Paper Goodies

| c | a | p | e |
|---|---|---|---|
| a | c | t | x |
| t | r | a | t |
| m | a | n | p |

- Cut out a _____ by _____ square of graph paper.
- In different places on the square, write in _____ words that contain the
  - ☐ short
  - ☐ long

  vowel sound _____.
- Give the puzzle to a friend to find your words.

Copyright © 2008 by John Wiley & Sons, Inc.

**Differentiated Instruction Made Easy**

# Phonics Task Cards *(continued)*

## Graph Paper Graphics

Cut out _____ strips of graph paper.
Make some _____ squares long.
Make others _____ squares long.
Use your _____ to find words
with the same number of letters. Use
words that have the _____ sound
at the _____ of the word. Paste
your word strips on a piece of paper.

| C | A | T |

| C | R | A | B |

## Long and Short

Cut out _____ strips of
graph paper of different lengths. Make
_____ words with the
☐ short      ☐ long
vowel sound _____.
Mix them up.

- Unscramble your strips. Make a long-
  vowel pile and a short-vowel pile.
- Give your strips to _____
  to unscramble into long- and short-
  vowel piles.

| f | a | t |

| f | a | t | e |

| m | a | n |

| m | a | n | e |

Copyright © 2008 by John Wiley & Sons, Inc.

# Phonics Task Cards *(continued)*

| | |
|---|---|
| **Keeping Tabs** | **How Does It End?** |

**Keeping Tabs**

Use _____ pages from _____.

☐ List words you find with short vowels.

☐ List words you find with long vowels.

☐ List words you find with blends.

☐ List words you find with silent E.

☐ List words you find with _____.

**How Does It End?**

☐ Look up

☐ Write

☐ Tape

☐ Tell

words that have the _____ ending.

• Use each word in a sentence.

• Make a flash card for each word.

• Write each word _____ times.

Copyright © 2008 by John Wiley & Sons. Inc.

# Phonics Activities

## Alphabet Bank

___a ___b ___c ___d ___e ___f ___g ___h ___i ___j

___k ___l ___m ___n ___o ___p ___q ___r ___s ___t

___u ___v ___w ___x ___y ___z

Copyright © 2008 by John Wiley & Sons, Inc.

☐ Each vowel is worth _____ cents.

☐ Give each consonant a value between 1 cent and _____ cents.

☐ Make up _____ words using the letters _____.

☐ How much is each word worth for your bank account?

☐ What word is
  ☐ most expensive?
  ☐ least expensive?

☐ Time yourself. How much money can you save in _____ minutes? Write as many words as you can in that time and total their worth.

☐ How many words can you make that cost exactly _____ cents?

# Phonics Activities *(continued)*

### Graph Paper Crosswords

Cut out _____ strips of graph paper. Paste them on a piece of paper in crossword puzzle form. Make a crossword puzzle using words with the _____ sound

- ☐ at the beginning
- ☐ in the middle
- ☐ at the end
- ☐ anywhere

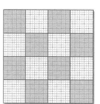

Copyright © 2008 by John Wiley & Sons, Inc.

# Book Report

Author _____

Title _____

Date completed _____

_____

_____

_____

_____

_____

_____

_____

_____

_____

_____

_____

_____

_____

_____

Copyright © 2008 by John Wiley & Sons. Inc.

# Book Report Tasks

☐   1. ☐ Write ☐ Record a _____ about the book.

☐   2. Describe _____ of the main characters.

☐   3. Create a new cover for the book.

☐   4. Create a
    ☐ TV ad       ☐ Newspaper ad      ☐ Diorama
    ☐ Radio ad    ☐ Poster           ☐ Video

☐   5. With _____, write about one day using characters from the book.

☐   6. _____ a sequel to the book.

☐   7. Create _____ new titles for the book.

☐   8. Make a puppet of your favorite character.

☐   9. Make pictures about your book. Mix up the pictures. Have a friend put them in the correct order.

☐ 10. ☐ Write ☐ Record a different ending for the book.

☐ 11. Create and perform a puppet show about the book ☐ by yourself ☐ with _____.

☐ 12. Pantomime a scene from the book.

☐ 13. ☐ Write ☐ Record a book review for the newspaper.

☐ 14. Pick a _____ from the book. List as many words you can think of to describe it.

☐ 15. Role-play a radio interview with the author of the book.

☐ 16. Make a costume for one of the characters in the book.

☐ 17. ☐ Write ☐ Record the part of the book you like best.

☐ 18. ☐ Write ☐ Record a story about the character
    ☐ You like best    ☐ You would like to be
    ☐ You like least   ☐ You would like to add to the book

☐ 19. Create some sound effects for your book.

☐ 20. Choose music to go with the book.

☐ 21. Read _____ of the book to _____.

☐ 22. Make a wanted poster for the villain of the book.

☐ 23. Make a comic strip about the book.

☐ 24. Draw a picture of a scene from the book. Cut it into a puzzle.
    ☐ Put it back together again.
    ☐ Give it to _____ to put together.

Copyright © 2008 by John Wiley & Sons. Inc.

# Book Report Tasks *(continued)*

- [ ] 25. Make a mobile about characters in the book.
- [ ] 26. [ ] Write [ ] Record
  - [ ] Events in the story that could *not* happen in real life.
  - [ ] Events in the story that *could* happen in real life.
  - [ ] Events you would *like* to have happen to you.
  - [ ] Events you would *not* like to have happen to you.
- [ ] 27. Create a timeline of events in the story.
- [ ] 28. Write a letter
  - [ ] To the author of the book, telling what you liked about it.
  - [ ] To a character in the book.
- [ ] 29. Create a news bulletin about the book.
- [ ] 30. Create a bookmark about the book.
- [ ] 31. Write a list of new words from the book.
- [ ] 32. Tell _____ about the book.
- [ ] 33. Read _____ book(s) by the same author.
- [ ] 34. Compose a song about the book.
- [ ] 35. Pretend you are a character in the book. [ ] Write [ ] Record [ ] Draw what you feel about what happens to you in the book.
- [ ] 36. Make a mobile about different settings in the book.
- [ ] 37. Create your own activity.

Copyright © 2008 by John Wiley & Sons, Inc.

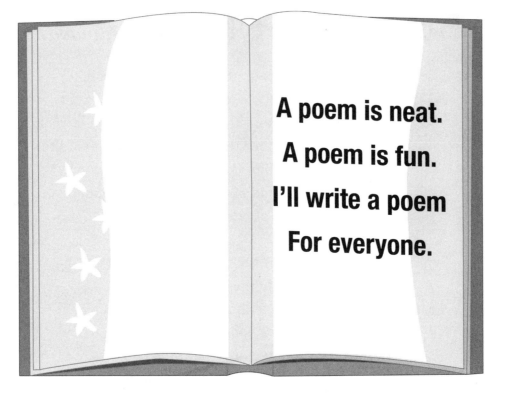

A poem is neat.

A poem is fun.

I'll write a poem

For everyone.

Copyright © 2008 by John Wiley & Sons. Inc.

# Poetry Contract

I, _____, agree to be

poet laureate for _____ tasks and will complete these tasks

by _____.

Date

_____

Teacher

_____

Poet Laureate

# Poetry Tasks

Now that you are ready to write poems:

☐   1. Make a list of as many words as you can think of that rhyme with _____.

☐   2. Choose a friend to rhyme with. Select _____ words and ask your friend to find rhymes for them. Then find rhymes for your friend's words.

☐   3. Select _____ words. Find _____ words that rhyme with each.

☐   4. Make _____ sets of flash cards with rhyming words. Put one word on each card. Then use your cards to:

    ☐ Match the words into rhyming pairs.

    ☐ Give your cards to _____ to match the rhyming words.

    ☐ Use your cards with a multilevel gameboard.

☐   5. Write _____ rhyming sentences using _____ of your words.

☐   6. Create a poem using _____ of your words.

    ☐ Write ☐ Type ☐ Recite ☐ Memorize

☐   7. Choose _____ kinds of poems.

    ☐ Find _____ examples of that kind of poem.

    ☐ Describe the ☐ rhyming ☐ theme ☐ style of the poem.

    ☐ Create a poem in the same style.

    ☐ Write ☐ Type ☐ Recite ☐ Memorize

☐   8. ☐ Write ☐ Type a poem about

    ☐ Your best friend     ☐ Your favorite _____

    ☐ Your pet     ☐ A color

    ☐ Nature     ☐ A film or TV star

    ☐ School     ☐ Your family

    ☐ A feeling     ☐ Your troubles

    ☐ A holiday     ☐ Other _____

Copyright © 2008 by John Wiley & Sons, Inc.

# Poetry Tasks *(continued)*

- ☐ 9. Select a poet.
  - ☐ Read _____ book(s) about the poet's life.
  - ☐ Write a description of
    - ☐ the poet
    - ☐ the poet's writing style
    - ☐ the subject(s) the poet writes about
  - ☐ Write a _____ in the style of the poet.
  - ☐ Read _____ poems written by this poet.
  - ☐ Write ☐ Type ☐ Illustrate one of the poet's poems.
- ☐ 10. ☐ Read ☐ Write ☐ Type a _____ poem.
  - ☐ Illustrate the poem.
  - ☐ Put the poem to music.
  - ☐ Memorize the poem.
  - ☐ Recite the poem to _____.
  - ☐ Create a greeting card with the poem.
  - ☐ Create a poster of the poem.
- ☐ 11. Design a poetry task of your choice! Have fun!

Copyright © 2008 by John Wiley & Sons, Inc.

# Chapter 2

# Spelling Activities

There is an art to teaching spelling to learners who are performing at various levels. The teacher's job need not include repetitive drill and practice, and endless explanations of the activities and tasks. The teacher should have various techniques and strategies at hand to teach spelling to the students' strengths. Learning to spell is not always easy, but it can certainly be simplified by using the contract and task cards included in this chapter. These innovations provide students with an individualized spelling approach that works in any classroom. The learner can achieve success without repetitious drilling. Every speller in the classroom, regardless of skill level, can use similar materials. The students will learn to make choices that are motivational and reinforcing. This can greatly reduce frustration and boredom.

Make multiple copies of the spelling contract. The students can use the same contract over and over. Their spelling words will change, and practice activities can vary. Once students get the hang of it, the teacher can spend time in direct instruction and not in direction giving. Task cards, flash cards, multilevel gameboards, and spinners can add to the excitement of learning in new ways. The number of tasks chosen by the student will vary. Some spellers will start with one task at a time. Remember, when we use the word *write* we are referring to a variety of methods. Computers, pencils, pens, crayons, sandwriting, clay, and other means can be used to teach and reinforce the skills required. In the end, your students will each have a greater understanding of the best way for them to learn, and you will be able to focus on direct teaching to individual needs while your classroom moves at a pace that works for all learners.

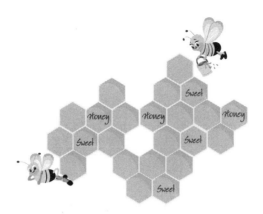

# Spelling Contract

Name _____

Date _____

Choose your method: ☐ Write   ☐ Keyboard   ☐ Other

## Word List

_____

_____

_____

_____

_____

_____

_____

_____

_____

   Cross out _____ of your spelling words. Replace them with words you would like to learn.

   I will choose _____ spelling tasks and complete _____ assigned tasks.

   I will complete this spelling contract on or before _____.

Contract Due Date

Copyright © 2008 by John Wiley & Sons, Inc.

# Spelling Tasks

Now that you have selected your spelling words:

- [ ] 1. Write each word _____ times.
- [ ] 2. Use each word in a sentence. ☐ Say it. ☐ Write it.
- [ ] 3. Write each word on the board _____ times.
- [ ] 4. Read and spell _____ words to a friend.
- [ ] 5. Use as many words as you can in one sentence. ☐ Say it. ☐ Write it.
- [ ] 6. Use _____ words in a ☐ story ☐ poem ☐ song ☐ other _____.
- [ ] 7. Underline the _____ in each word.
- [ ] 8. Circle the _____ in each word.
- [ ] 9. Divide _____ words into syllables.
- [ ] 10. Look up _____ words in a dictionary and write the definitions.
- [ ] 11. Write ☐ synonyms ☐ antonyms for _____ words.
- [ ] 12. Write all the _____ syllable words.
- [ ] 13. Create _____ new words by adding ☐ pre ☐ dis ☐ re ☐ de ☐ in to the beginning of your words.
- [ ] 14. Create new words by adding ☐ s ☐ es ☐ ing ☐ ed ☐ er ☐ ly ☐ _____, ☐ _____, ☐ _____ to the end of your words.
- [ ] 15. Write the words that start with _____.
- [ ] 16. Write the words that end with _____.
- [ ] 17. Write the words that have short vowel sounds.
- [ ] 18. Write the words that have long vowel sounds.
- [ ] 19. Choose _____ of your favorite words. ☐ Tell why. ☐ Draw why. ☐ Write why.

Copyright © 2008 by John Wiley & Sons, Inc.

# Spelling Tasks *(continued)*

- ☐ 20. Create a spelling game and play it with _____ friends.
- ☐ 21. Put your words in ABC order.
- ☐ 22. Draw a picture for _____ words.
- ☐ 23. Make up a secret code for _____ of your words. See if a friend can solve the code.
- ☐ 24. Work for _____ minutes in a computer spelling program.
- ☐ 25. Create a skit using _____ of your words. Have your friends help you act it out.
- ☐ 26. Play charades with _____ of your words.
- ☐ 27. Write each word on a flash card. Study the cards with a friend.
- ☐ 28. Make a picture dictionary for _____ of your words.
- ☐ 29. Have a friend test you on _____ of your words.
- ☐ 30. Take a pretest with _____.
- ☐ 31. Take a final test with _____.
- ☐ 32. Correct your own work.
- ☐ 33. Select _____ spelling task cards and complete the tasks.
- ☐ 34. Choose _____ spelling activities yourself.

Copyright © 2008 by John Wiley & Sons, Inc.

**Differentiated Instruction Made Easy**

# Spelling Task Cards

Write words _____ times in the air. Make them BIG.

Think about how you learn your words. Teach _____ words to a friend.

Spell words to _____.

Say, spell, and write each word _____ times.

Write words _____ times on the board.

Trace and say _____ words _____ times.

Copyright © 2008 by John Wiley & Sons, Inc.

**Spelling Activities**

# Spelling Task Cards *(continued)*

Have _____ spell words to you. Say what they are.

Compose a song or poem using _____ of your spelling words.

Write your words _____ times ☐ in sand ☐ out of clay ☐ other _____.

Look at a word. Turn it over and write it from memory. Do this with _____ words.

Find _____ words in a book, newspaper, magazine, or _____.

Find pictures and words to describe _____ of your words. Make a collage.

Copyright © 2008 by John Wiley & Sons. Inc.

**Differentiated Instruction Made Easy**

# Spelling Flash Cards

*Note to teacher:* Duplicate these pages. Students can cut out the cards and make their own flash cards for use with contracts, task cards, and gameboards.

Copyright © 2008 by John Wiley & Sons, Inc.

# Spelling Flash Cards *(continued)*

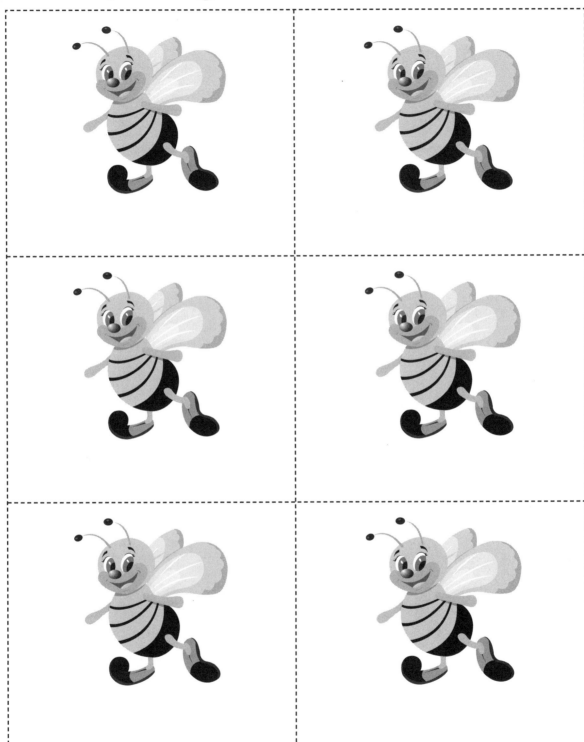

Copyright © 2008 by John Wiley & Sons, Inc.

**Differentiated Instruction Made Easy**

# Chapter 3

# Writing Activities

This chapter provides ideas for supporting student creativity across a variety of genres—fiction, nonfiction, poetry, scripts, recordings, cartoons, comics, and so on. Your writing program can be individualized or it can support group projects such as developing a TV program or film. Opportunities are plentiful to keep motivation high while increasing writing skills and generalizing to other content areas.

The following pages provide multilevel written-language contracts, creative idea cards, wheels, script paper, storyboard paper, and diary sheets.

The contracts, diary sheets, and script paper can be duplicated and used to write scripts and plan camera shots for possible TV shows or films. The storyboard paper can be used to plan, write, and illustrate books, filmstrips, and so forth.

The creative idea cards can be laminated and used in activity centers or along with an individual contract. The spinners and wheels can be used in various combinations to support students' creativity.

# A Dear _____ Contract

Dear _____,

I, _____, agree to complete

_____ letter-writing tasks by _____.

I will ☐ write ☐ keyboard these activities.

Sincerely,

_____

Copyright © 2008 by John Wiley & Sons, Inc.

# Writing Tasks

☐ 1. Write a friendly letter to _____.

☐ 2. ☐ Write ☐ Type a business letter to a company.

☐ 3. Write a thank-you note to _____.

☐ 4. Write a letter to the president of _____.

☐ 5. Write a letter applying for a job.

☐ 6. Write a letter of recommendation for _____.

☐ 7. Write a letter answering a classified ad in the newspaper.

☐ 8. Write a fan letter.

☐ 9. Write a get-well letter.

☐ 10. Design a greeting card: ☐ birthday ☐ holiday ☐ your choice.

☐ 11. Design your own stationery and envelopes.

☐ 12. Design an invitation to a _____.

☐ 13. Write a letter to a ☐ politician ☐ hero ☐ other to share something special about yourself.

☐ 14. Create a letter using pictures only.

☐ 15. Design a stamp honoring a ☐ person ☐ place ☐ holiday.

☐ 16. Choose a secret pal. Write a friendly letter to that person.

☐ 17. Write a cheery letter to someone in a ☐ hospital ☐ home for seniors.

☐ 18. List the parts of a business letter.

☐ 19. Make a poster showing the different parts of a letter.

☐ 20. Begin a stamp collection.

☐ 21. Write an imaginary postcard from _____.

☐ 22. Design a postcard.

☐ 23. Send a postcard to _____.

Copyright © 2008 by John Wiley & Sons, Inc.

# Writing Tasks *(continued)*

☐ 24. Find out how much postage you need to send a ☐ letter ☐ postcard to ☐ USA ☐ another country.

☐ 25. Go on a field trip to a post office.

☐ 26. Teach _____ how to write a letter.

☐ 27. Ask _____ to be your secretary. Dictate a letter.

☐ 28. Record a letter.

☐ 29. Write a letter accepting an invitation to _____.

☐ 30. Write a letter giving directions to _____ from _____.

☐ 31. Write a letter of sympathy to _____ for _____.

Copyright © 2008 by John Wiley & Sons, Inc.

# Creative Expression Contract

Title of Creation: _____

I, _____, hereby agree to:

- ☐ 1. Write
- ☐ 2. Illustrate
- ☐ 3. Make an audio recording
- ☐ 4. Make a video recording
- ☐ 5. Dictate

- ☐ 6. Compose
- ☐ 7. Keyboard
- ☐ 8. Photograph
- ☐ 9. _____

I will create:

- ☐ 1. _____ Poems
- ☐ 2. _____ Sentences
- ☐ 3. _____ Paragraphs
- ☐ 4. _____ Script
- ☐ 5. Biography of _____
- ☐ 6. Autobiography
- ☐ 7. Journal
- ☐ 8. Speech
- ☐ 9. Essay
- ☐ 10. _____ books

- ☐ 11. Composition
- ☐ 12. Song
- ☐ 13. Cartoon
- ☐ 14. Comic strip
- ☐ 15. Graffiti collection
- ☐ 16. Letter to _____
- ☐ 17. Article for newspaper
- ☐ 18. Article for magazine
- ☐ 19. Web page _____

I will need:

- ☐ 1. Writing paper
- ☐ 2. Typing paper
- ☐ 3. Script paper
- ☐ 4. Storyboard paper
- ☐ 5. Diary paper
- ☐ 6. Staff paper (for music)
- ☐ 7. Art paper
- ☐ 8. Art supplies: _____
- ☐ 9. Envelope
- ☐ 10. Stamp

- ☐ 11. Audio recorder
- ☐ 12. Video recorder
- ☐ 13. Camera
- ☐ 14. Computer
- ☐ 15. Pen or pencil
- ☐ 16. Idea cards
- ☐ 17. Idea spinner
- ☐ 18. Idea contract
- ☐ 19. Other: _____

Signed: _____

Date completed: _____

Copyright © 2008 by John Wiley & Sons, Inc.

# Creative Idea Cards

**FLASH!** There's a new country and we need some signs for it.

☐ Write ☐ Tell ☐ Tape ☐ Draw ☐ Make
  ☐ Signs we need
  ☐ Signs we do NOT need
  ☐ New signs you would like to see
  ☐ Signs for
    ☐ Pets ☐ Monsters
    ☐ Children ☐ Space creatures
    ☐ Adults
    ☐ Other _____

**SPECIAL!** You are the winner! You have just won a _____.

☐ Write ☐ Tell ☐ Tape ☐ Draw ☐ Act out
  ☐ How you feel
  ☐ What you will do with it
  ☐ If or how it will change your life
  ☐ What you will need now that you did not need before you won it
  ☐ How and with whom you can share it

**EUREKA!** You have really done it now! You've come up with a brand-new invention.

☐ Write ☐ Tell ☐ Tape ☐ Draw ☐ Build
  ☐ A nonsense invention
  ☐ An invention we really need around here
  ☐ An invention to help us in outer space
  ☐ An invention to help us in dinosaur land
  ☐ An invention for people to help each other
  ☐ An invention to _____

**SMILE!** You're on TV!

☐ Write ☐ Tell ☐ Tape ☐ Draw ☐ Act out
  ☐ A campaign spot to get _____

  elected to _____
  ☐ A commercial to sell
    ☐ Yourself
    ☐ A product called _____
    ☐ A public service spot for the news. Make your news
    ☐ good ☐ funny ☐ realistic
    ☐ impossible.

Copyright © 2008 by John Wiley & Sons. Inc.

# Creative Idea Cards *(continued)*

**HEAR YE!** The teller of tall tales is here.

□ Write □ Tell □ Tape □ Draw □ Act out
- □ The biggest whopper you can think of
- □ A tall tale that could really happen, if you were lucky
- □ A tall tale that could NOT happen in a million years
- □ A tall tale you would like to see happen
- □ A tale you would be scared to see happen

**ENTER NOW!** Hurry. Quickly—before the deadline.

□ Write □ Tell □ Tape □ Draw □ Act out
- □ The kind of contest you would like to enter
- □ _____ of the rules
- □ What the prizes are
  - □ First prize _____
  - □ Second prize _____
  - □ Other _____
- □ Enter a real contest

Copyright © 2008 by John Wiley & Sons. Inc.

# My Journal

Name: _____

Day of the Week: _____ Date: _____

Dear Journal:

_____

_____

_____

_____

_____

_____

_____

How I feel today:

_____

_____

_____

_____

_____

_____

_____

_____

Copyright © 2008 by John Wiley & Sons, Inc.

**Differentiated Instruction Made Easy**

# Chapter 4

# Math Activities

Although we recognize the importance of math in our students' lives, we know that many students enjoy learning math while others find math challenging. How can teachers address the many interests and achievement levels within one classroom?

The multilevel math materials offered here may be used to help all learners. The activities may be customized for each student, enabling the teacher to reach students with different levels of math achievement within the classroom. They may be used with individual students or with groups of students. Included are tasks for drill and practice, problem solving, creative thinking, and cooperative learning. They are designed to complement traditionally sequenced math programs.

# Funny Money Contract

I, _____, hereby agree to complete _____

Funny Money tasks of my choosing and to accept responsibility for _____

tasks assigned to me. I can use my brain power alone or I can also solve these

money problems with a ☐ calculator ☐ computer ☐ other _____.

These tasks will be completed by _____.
<br>Date

_____
<br>Teacher

_____
<br>Student

Copyright © 2008 by John Wiley & Sons, Inc.

# Funny Money Tasks

Now that you have completed the Funny Money Contract, you may work on the following tasks:

☐ 1. Make a ☐ collage ☐ scrapbook ☐ bulletin board ☐ other _____ to illustrate _____ ways in which you can use money.

☐ 2. Make a ☐ collage ☐ scrapbook ☐ bulletin board ☐ other _____ to illustrate things that money cannot buy.

☐ 3. Using a ☐ catalog ☐ newspaper ☐ Web site ☐ other _____, choose _____ items you would like to purchase. ☐ Add the total amount. ☐ Add a _____ percent sales tax.

☐ 4. Make rubbings of both sides of all U.S. coins. ☐ Label the coins. ☐ Write the coins' values. ☐ Describe the symbols on the coins.

☐ 5. Choose an item you would like to purchase from a ☐ newspaper ☐ a catalog ☐ the Internet ☐ other _____. Compare the prices by creating a bar graph.

☐ 6. Using a ☐ catalog ☐ newspaper ☐ Web site ☐ other _____, make a list of what you would buy if you had $ _____.

☐ 7. Design your own money.

☐ 8. Make up _____ word problems using ☐ addition ☐ subtraction ☐ multiplication ☐ division ☐ other _____. Solve these problems yourself and then ☐ ask a friend to solve them ☐ ask your class to solve them. Were the solutions the same or different? Explain.

☐ 9. You have just won $_____! What will you do with this money? Will you save it, spend it, donate it, or use it in another way? ☐ Write ☐ Tell about your plan.

☐ 10. Using a menu from a local restaurant, plan to take _____ friends or family members out for a meal. What would the total cost be? ☐ Add a _____ percent tip.

☐ 11. Create _____ activities that will help you learn more about money. Have fun!

Copyright © 2008 by John Wiley & Sons, Inc.

**Math Activities**                                                        **39**

# Funny Money Tasks *(continued)*

☐ 12. With _____ friends, set up a store. Put prices on the items. Open for business. ☐ Write ☐ Tell _____ things you learned about this process.

☐ 13. Plan a classroom auction using _____ donated items. Calculate how much money the class earned. Describe what your class will do with the money and why the class decided to use the money in that way.

☐ 14. Go to a bank and get samples of ☐ a check ☐ a deposit slip ☐ a savings account book ☐ other _____. ☐ Write ☐ Tell how to use them.

☐ 15. Practice what you have learned about banking. Design and create a banking system for your classroom. Create the ☐ money ☐ the checks ☐ the deposit slip ☐ a savings account book ☐ other _____.

☐ 16. Imagine that you can go on a vacation of your dreams ☐ by yourself ☐ with _____ friends. Make a list of what you would need to buy in order to go on this vacation. Hint: be sure to include transportation expenses! Use the ☐ Internet ☐ a travel agency ☐ a newspaper ☐ other _____ to determine how much your vacation would cost.

☐ 17. Study the money system from another country. Find _____ items in ☐ a catalog ☐ in a newspaper ☐ on the Internet and convert the prices to the money system for that country.

☐ 18. Collect ☐ pennies ☐ other coins in the largest jar you can find. Estimate how many coins are in the jar after _____ days. Create a chart or graph of your estimates. Donate the money to a local charity.

Copyright © 2008 by John Wiley & Sons, Inc.

**Differentiated Instruction Made Easy**

# Math Contract

Name: _____ Date: _____

I hereby agree to complete _____ tasks of my choosing and _____

assigned tasks on or before _____.

Write your math facts here:

_____

_____

_____

_____

_____

_____

_____

_____

_____

Copyright © 2008 by John Wiley & Sons, Inc.

# Math Tasks

☐  1. Write your math facts _____ times ☐ on paper
☐ on the board ☐ on flash cards (with answers on the back)
☐ on the computer ☐ other _____ .

☐  2. Say each fact _____ times to ☐ a friend
☐ other _____ .

☐  3. Write _____ story problems using
_____ of your facts.

☐  4. Write the facts that are easiest for you to remember.

☐  5. Write the facts that challenge your brain—the hard ones!

☐  6. Make a spinner with your facts on it.

☐  7. Choose a multilevel gameboard and invent a math practice game.

☐  8. Design a game that will help you remember your facts. Play
the game with _____ friends.

☐  9. Invent a secret code using your math facts.

☐ 10. Switch flash cards with a ☐ friend ☐ teacher ☐ family
member and practice your facts.

☐ 11. Play a game of tic-tac-toe with a friend, but write _____
facts correctly before each move. Try using other games such
as checkers and dominoes in the same way.

Copyright © 2008 by John Wiley & Sons. Inc.

# Math Tasks (continued)

☐ 12. Use the computer to type your facts.

☐ 13. ☐ Add ☐ Subtract ☐ Multiply ☐ Divide using the number
_____ and your math facts.

☐ 14. Have a friend test your math facts and keep a record of your
progress for _____ days.

☐ 15. Use the calculator to ☐ practice your facts ☐ check your
work.

☐ 16. Invent _____ practice activities for ☐ yourself
☐ a friend.

☐ 17. Using the music from one of your favorite songs, create a new
song that includes your math facts. Make a recording of your
new song.

☐ 18. Take a break to clear your head for _____
minutes.

☐ 19. Create _____ math tasks ☐ for yourself
☐ for a friend ☐ for your class.

Copyright © 2008 by John Wiley & Sons. Inc.

# Story Problem Wheels

Each of the following wheels has eight statements. Personalize each statement by adding the names of your students. By combining the smaller and the larger wheels with a spinner, you can generate sixty-four story problems. Multiply that by accompanying task cards and you have hundreds of problems to choose from. Exchange a wheel with the one on another page and you have hundreds more!

# Story Problem Wheels *(continued)*

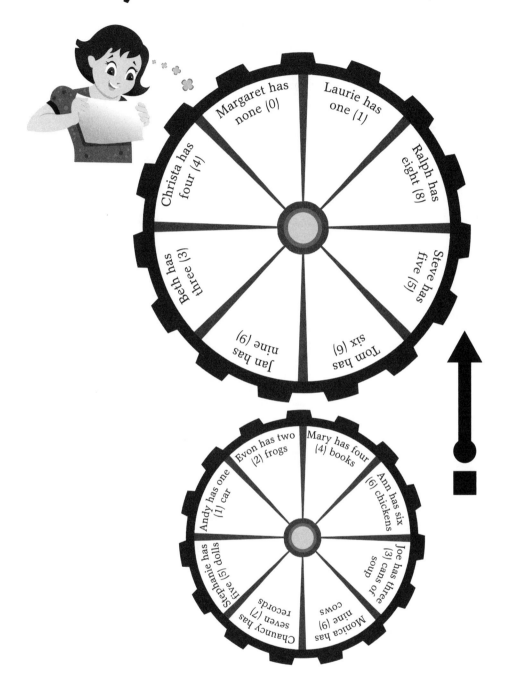

*Note to teacher:* Wheels may be enlarged as appropriate to the grade level.

Copyright © 2008 by John Wiley & Sons, Inc.

# Story Problem Wheels *(continued)*

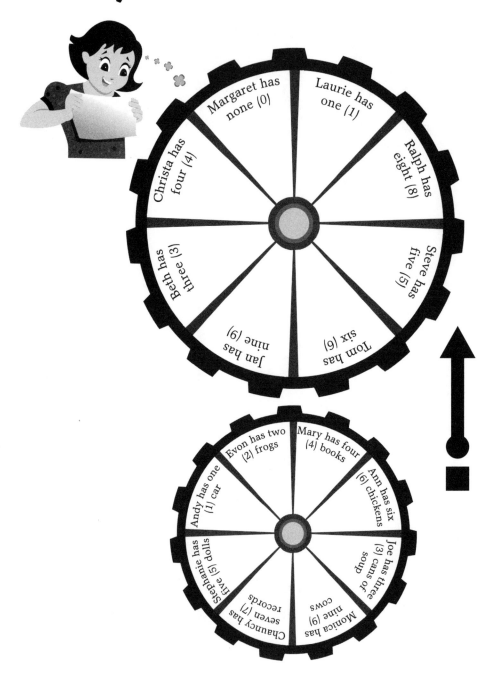

*Note to teacher:* Wheels may be enlarged as appropriate to the grade level.

Copyright © 2008 by John Wiley & Sons, Inc.

**Differentiated Instruction Made Easy**

# Story Problem Task Cards

Use these task cards with the story problem wheels.

+ − × ÷

Who has more?

+ − × ÷

Who has less?

+ − × ÷

Who has more—and
how many more?

+ − × ÷

Who has less—and how
many less?

+ − × ÷

Divide their total by
_____. How
many do they have now?

+ − × ÷

Multiply their total by
_____. How
many do they have now?

+ − × ÷

Another friend
comes along with
_____ more.
What is the total now?

+ − × ÷

Someone comes and
takes _____
away. How many do they
have now?

+ − × ÷

In a year, they will have
_____ % more.
How many will they
have then?

Copyright © 2008 by John Wiley & Sons. Inc.

**Math Activities**

# Arithmetic Task Cards

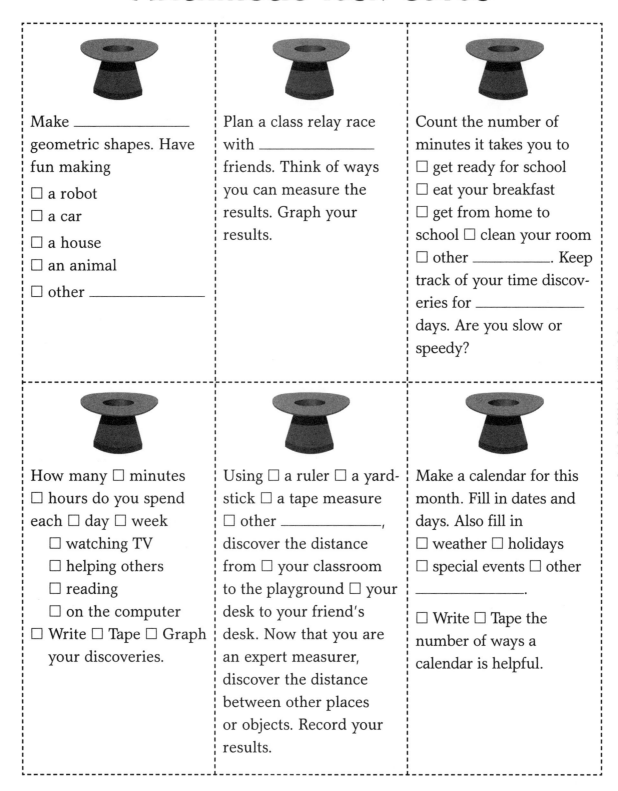

Make _____ geometric shapes. Have fun making
☐ a robot
☐ a car
☐ a house
☐ an animal
☐ other _____

Plan a class relay race with _____ friends. Think of ways you can measure the results. Graph your results.

Count the number of minutes it takes you to
☐ get ready for school
☐ eat your breakfast
☐ get from home to school ☐ clean your room
☐ other _____. Keep track of your time discoveries for _____ days. Are you slow or speedy?

How many ☐ minutes ☐ hours do you spend each ☐ day ☐ week
   ☐ watching TV
   ☐ helping others
   ☐ reading
   ☐ on the computer
☐ Write ☐ Tape ☐ Graph your discoveries.

Using ☐ a ruler ☐ a yardstick ☐ a tape measure ☐ other _____, discover the distance from ☐ your classroom to the playground ☐ your desk to your friend's desk. Now that you are an expert measurer, discover the distance between other places or objects. Record your results.

Make a calendar for this month. Fill in dates and days. Also fill in
☐ weather ☐ holidays
☐ special events ☐ other _____.

☐ Write ☐ Tape the number of ways a calendar is helpful.

Copyright © 2008 by John Wiley & Sons, Inc.

# Arithmetic Task Cards *(continued)*

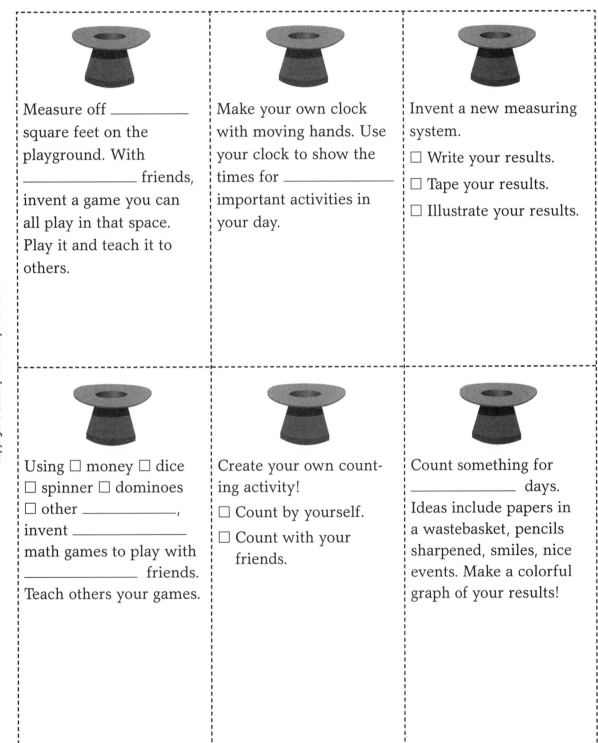

Measure off _____ square feet on the playground. With _____ friends, invent a game you can all play in that space. Play it and teach it to others.

Make your own clock with moving hands. Use your clock to show the times for _____ important activities in your day.

Invent a new measuring system.
☐ Write your results.
☐ Tape your results.
☐ Illustrate your results.

Using ☐ money ☐ dice ☐ spinner ☐ dominoes ☐ other _____, invent _____ math games to play with _____ friends. Teach others your games.

Create your own counting activity!
☐ Count by yourself.
☐ Count with your friends.

Count something for _____ days. Ideas include papers in a wastebasket, pencils sharpened, smiles, nice events. Make a colorful graph of your results!

Copyright © 2008 by John Wiley & Sons. Inc.

**Math Activities**

# Arithmetic Task Cards *(continued)*

With _____ friends, collect all sorts of buttons. Sort them by size, shape, color. Think of other ways to sort them. How many different ways did you discover? Now look around and find other things that you can sort. Sorting is fun!
☐ Graph your results.
☐ Illustrate your results.
☐ Write about your results.

What are your class-mates' favorite
☐ foods?
☐ songs?
☐ sports?
☐ teams?
☐ TV shows?
☐ other _____
☐ Write ☐ Tape a report about your survey.

How are we alike and different? Choose _____ friends.
☐ Count. ☐ Compare.
☐ Graph your findings. What do you discover when you investigate
☐ hair color
☐ eye color
☐ birth month
☐ other _____?

How many times a day do ☐ you ☐ your teacher ☐ your friend ☐ laugh ☐ say something nice ☐ get mad ☐ feel happy ☐ feel sad ☐ other _____.

Count and graph this for _____ days.

Invent your own clock activity.

Create your own math activity.

Copyright © 2008 by John Wiley & Sons, Inc.

# Chapter 5

# History Activities

The multilevel history experiences offered in this chapter are designed to extend and support traditional topics and core curricula. Students should be encouraged to choose subject matter that is of interest to them. History contracts, travel brochures, and news pages accommodate a wide range of learning styles and are designed to stimulate curiosity and enhance students' research skills.

Although these activities can be used with individuals, many are also appropriate for learning centers or with small groups of students.

# The Historical Person Contract

The famous person I have chosen is:

_____.

   The life of this person fascinates me because _____

_____

_____.

   I will choose _____ historical tasks and will complete

_____ assigned tasks.

   I will finish this Historical Person Contract on or before _____.

                                                                      Date

_____
               Teacher

_____
       Official Historian

Copyright © 2008 by John Wiley & Sons, Inc.

# Historical Person: Fact-Finding Activities

Use ☐ your history book ☐ an encyclopedia ☐ library resources ☐ the Internet ☐ a video ☐ newspapers and magazines to complete the following tasks:

☐ 1. Create a memory book in which to put your historical information, *or* organize a ☐ file folder ☐ box ☐ computer file.

☐ 2. In your memory book, folder, box, or file, include the following information:

    ☐ Date and place of birth of this person

    ☐ Date and place of death (if applicable)

    ☐ Places where this person lived

    ☐ Facts about this person's childhood and family

    ☐ Facts about this person's adult life and family

    ☐ Information about this person's special interests and hobbies

    ☐ Information about this person's outstanding contributions to

        ☐ society ☐ other _____.

☐ 3. Use your creative skills to decorate or organize your memory book, folder, box, or file.

Copyright © 2008 by John Wiley & Sons, Inc.

**History Activities**

# Historical Person Tasks

Now that you have gathered this information:

☐ 1. ☐ Write ☐ Illustrate ☐ Make an audio recording ☐ Make a video recording ☐ Tell ☐ Make a map ☐ Other _____ to demonstrate your knowledge of _____.

☐ 2. Make a historical timeline of your famous person's life and insert _____ historical facts on it.

☐ 3. ☐ Write a poem ☐ Make up a song or rap ☐ Create a skit ☐ Create a comic strip ☐ Illustrate to show important events in the life of your historical person.

☐ 4. Find out about _____ other historical persons who lived during the time your person was alive. Were any of these people friends of your person? Enter this information in your historical memory book.

☐ 5. Imagine that you are your historical person. ☐ Write a letter ☐ Make a phone call ☐ Send an e-mail that he or she would have written, made, or sent.

☐ 6. With _____ friends, create a skit about this person. ☐ Make costumes ☐ Design sets ☐ Other _____ for your performance.

☐ 7. Make ☐ a postage stamp ☐ a poster ☐ a flag ☐ other _____ that honors this famous person.

☐ 8. Create a diorama ☐ Produce a video ☐ Create a Web site ☐ Other _____ about an important event in your historical person's life.

☐ 9. ☐ Write ☐ Make an audio recording ☐ Make a video recording ☐ Illustrate situations and events during which your historical person felt ☐ happy ☐ sad ☐ competitive ☐ proud ☐ other emotions _____.

Copyright © 2008 by John Wiley & Sons. Inc.

# Historical Person Tasks *(continued)*

Copyright © 2008 by John Wiley & Sons. Inc.

☐ 10. ☐ Write ☐ Make an audio recording ☐ Make a video recording
☐ Illustrate ☐ Other _____ information about
the reason for your historical person's fame. Did this person
discover or invent something? Did this person contribute great
ideas and ideals to society? Why did you choose this person?

☐ 11. Imagine that you are this person. ☐ Journal ☐ Make an audio
recording ☐ Make a video recording ☐ Illustrate your thoughts
for _____ days. Ask your teacher for a journal
format you can use.

☐ 12. Make a ☐ game ☐ task wheel ☐ task card and teach
_____ friends about this person's life and
contributions.

☐ 13. Pretend that you are your historical person. Have someone
interview you. Record the interview and share it with
_____ friends.

**History Activities**

# The Historical Invention Contract

Things all around me, a thousand and one,
And now I am wondering from where did they come?
The car didn't grow in a garden so green,
And whose idea was the ice cream machine?

I, _____, want to learn about the invention and development of

_____ because _____

_____

_____ .

    I will complete _____ assigned tasks and _____

tasks of my own choosing by _____ .
                                        Date

_____
        Teacher

_____
        Official Historian

Copyright © 2008 by John Wiley & Sons, Inc.

# Historical Invention: Fact-Finding Activities

Use ☐ your history book ☐ an encyclopedia ☐ library resources ☐ the Internet ☐ a video ☐ newspapers and magazines ☐ interview of a knowledgeable person from an organization that manufactures your invention to learn about the invention. Then complete the following tasks:

☐ 1. Create a memory book in which you can put the information about your historical invention, *or* organize a ☐ file folder ☐ box ☐ computer file.

☐ 2. In your memory book, folder, box, or file, include the following information:

    ☐ Date and place of origin

    ☐ Inventor

    ☐ Historical facts about the invention

    ☐ Modern-day facts about and improvements to the invention

    ☐ Historical and modern uses for the invention

    ☐ What people did before this invention

    ☐ Other _____

☐ 3. Use your creative skills to decorate or organize your memory book, folder, box, or file.

Copyright © 2008 by John Wiley & Sons, Inc.

**History Activities**

**57**

# Historical Invention Tasks

Now that you have collected this information:

☐ 1. ☐ Write ☐ Tell ☐ Make an audio recording ☐ Make a video recording ☐ Illustrate the information about your invention.

☐ 2. ☐ Write a poem ☐ Perform a skit ☐ Make a poster ☐ Draw a cartoon about your invention.

☐ 3. Create a timeline that shows your invention's growth and development.

☐ 4. Design a ☐ stamp ☐ flag ☐ advertisement that describes your invention and its inventor.

☐ 5. Imagine that you are the inventor of this wonderful invention. ☐ Write ☐ Make an audio recording ☐ Make a video recording

☐ Keep a diary for _____ days about your life as the clever and talented inventor.

☐ 6. Create a collage that tells about your ☐ historical invention ☐ your modern invention.

☐ 7. Create a prototype of this invention out of _____.

☐ 8. Design an award that you would give to the inventor.

☐ 9. Teach _____ friends about your invention. Make a ☐ task wheel ☐ game ☐ task cards ☐ other _____ that will help your friends learn about this invention.

☐ 10. What emotion did this invention make you feel? Present this emotion in your own creative way.

Copyright © 2008 by John Wiley & Sons, Inc.

**Differentiated Instruction Made Easy**

Copyright © 2008 by John Wiley & Sons. Inc.

# The Historical Travel Contract

I, _____, hereby agree to turn back the hands of time in order to

visit a historical ☐ place ☐ artifact that is known as _____. On

this imaginary trip I will complete  historical discovery tasks of my choice and

_____ assigned tasks. This ancient adventure will be completed

on or before the modern day of _____.

                    Date


_____

           Teacher


_____

        Official Historian

# Historical Travel: Fact-Finding Activities

Use ☐ your history book ☐ an encyclopedia ☐ library resources ☐ the Internet ☐ a video ☐ newspapers and magazines ☐ interview a knowledgeable person ☐ other _____ to learn about your historical place or artifact. Then complete the following tasks:

☐ 1. Create a memory book in which you can put the information about your historical place or artifact, *or* organize a ☐ file folder ☐ box ☐ computer file.

☐ 2. In your memory book, folder, box, or file, include the following information:

    ☐ Important dates in the life of the historical place or artifact

    ☐ Historical persons associated with the place or artifact

    ☐ Historical facts about the place or artifact

    ☐ Modern-day facts about the place or artifact

    ☐ Your reasons for selecting the place or artifact

    ☐ Other _____

☐ 3. Use your creative skills to decorate or organize your memory book, folder, box, or file.

Copyright © 2008 by John Wiley & Sons, Inc.

# Historical Travel Tasks

Now that you have collected this information:

☐ 1. Pretend that you will take a trip to your historical site. Call, visit a travel agent, or use the Internet to find out the following information:

    ☐ Cost of the trip

    ☐ Climate

    ☐ Accommodations

    ☐ Other _____

☐ 2. Design a travel brochure that will encourage others to take this trip.

☐ 3. Design and create ☐ a poster ☐ audio recording ☐ advertisement ☐ postage stamp ☐ flag that teaches others about this historical place or artifact.

☐ 4. ☐ Write ☐ Illustrate your own book about this historical site or artifact.

☐ 5. Create a ☐ game ☐ task wheel ☐ task cards that will teach _____ others about your historical site or artifact.

☐ 6. Create a replica of your historical site or artifact.

☐ 7. Using your map skills, complete the following tasks:

    ☐ Find your historical site on a map.

    ☐ Draw your own map out of _____ that illustrates the location of this site or artifact.

    ☐ Locate nearby historical sites and artifacts on your map.

☐ 8. ☐ Write ☐ Illustrate ☐ Make an audio recording ☐ Make a video recording ☐ Other _____ what life was like in this historical spot _____ years ago.

☐ 9. Pretend that you are going to this part of the world for _____ days. Plan an itinerary and keep a travel log.

☐ 10. ☐ Write ☐ Illustrate how you feel about this historical site or artifact.

Copyright © 2008 by John Wiley & Sons. Inc.

# The Historical Event Contract

The historical event I have chosen is _____.

This event is interesting to me because _____

_____

_____.

I will complete _____ historical event tasks of my choice and

_____ assigned tasks by _____.
Date

_____
Teacher

_____
Official Historian

Copyright © 2008 by John Wiley & Sons. Inc.

# Historical Event: Fact-Finding Activities

Use ☐ your history book ☐ an encyclopedia ☐ library resources ☐ the Internet ☐ a video ☐ newspapers and magazines ☐ interview of a knowledgeable person ☐ other _____ to learn about your historical event. Then complete the following tasks:

☐ 1. Create an organizer in which to store your historical information:
    ☐ Box ☐ File folder ☐ Computer file ☐ Binder ☐ Memory book
    ☐ Other _____

☐ 2. In your organizer, include the following information:
    ☐ Name or title of event
    ☐ Date of event
    ☐ Where it happened
    ☐ Who was involved
    ☐ What happened

☐ 3. Decorate and organize your organizer.

☐ 4. Use your organizer with _____ of the following tasks.

Copyright © 2008 by John Wiley & Sons, Inc.

# Historical Event Tasks

Now that you have gathered this information:

☐ 1. ☐ Write ☐ Illustrate ☐ Make an audio recording ☐ Make a video recording ☐ Draw a map about what caused the event to happen.

☐ 2. Create a historical timeline of the event. Illustrate the timeline.

☐ 3. Imagine you are present at this event. ☐ Write a letter ☐ Send a text message ☐ Make a phone call ☐ Send an e-mail to someone about what is happening.

☐ 4. Create a diary about the event.

☐ 5. Describe what happened as a result of the event. ☐ Write ☐ Illustrate ☐ Make an audio recording ☐ Make a video recording

☐ 6. Describe why you think the event took place. ☐ Write ☐ Illustrate ☐ Make an audio recording ☐ Make an video recording

☐ 7. Do you think the event benefited the world? Why or why not? ☐ Write ☐ Illustrate ☐ Make an audio recording ☐ Make a video recording

☐ 8. Make a ☐ game ☐ task wheel ☐ task cards about this event and share them with ☐ friends ☐ the class.

☐ 9. Create a skit about this event. Act it out with ☐ friends ☐ for the class ☐ for the whole school.

☐ 10. Design a ☐ poster ☐ postage stamp ☐ diorama ☐ collage.

☐ 11. Produce ☐ a video ☐ a book ☐ an art portfolio ☐ a Web site that tells about the event.

☐ 12. Compose a ☐ song ☐ rap ☐ poem about the event.

☐ 13. Develop a crossword puzzle using words that describe the event.

☐ 14. Plan ☐ an awards ceremony ☐ a party ☐ an article to honor the people involved in the event.

☐ 15. After learning about the event, how did you feel about it? Present your emotions in your own creative way.

☐ 16. What is your favorite event in ☐ entertainment ☐ sports ☐ school ☐ your neighborhood ☐ your city ☐ your family? Choose someone important to that event.

☐ 17. Imagine a future event you would like to happen such as ☐ world peace ☐ end of hunger in the world ☐ a medical cure

☐ other _____. Describe it in your own way.

Copyright © 2008 by John Wiley & Sons, Inc.

# Chapter 6

# Geography Activities

Using textbooks to teach geography often makes it difficult for students with a wide range of interests and reading levels to learn the content. The worksheets, contracts, and task cards in this chapter provide students with easy access to content using both self-selected and teacher-selected activities.

These worksheets and contracts can be used in a variety of ways. They can help students to work individually or in cooperative groups.

# Map About Me

I will complete one of the following maps:

☐ My classroom                ☐ My country

☐ My bedroom                  ☐ My world

☐ My route to school          ☐ My hemisphere

☐ My neighborhood             ☐ State of _____

☐ My city                     ☐ Country: _____

☐ My state                    ☐ Other _____

by _____
        Date

_____
        Teacher

_____
        Mapmaker

Copyright © 2008 by John Wiley & Sons, Inc.

Name _____  Date _____

# My Map

Copyright © 2008 by John Wiley & Sons. Inc.

# The Fifty States

I will complete _____ mapping activities and _____

assigned tasks by _____.
                              Date


_____
           Teacher


_____
        Official Historian

Copyright © 2008 by John Wiley & Sons, Inc.

**Differentiated Instruction Made Easy**

# The Fifty States Directions

☐ 1. Select a map of the United States from one of the following
sources:

☐ the Internet    ☐ this book    ☐ other

☐ 2. Use the map for the following tasks.

Copyright © 2008 by John Wiley & Sons. Inc.

# The Fifty States Tasks

☐ 1. Fill in the names of the states.

☐ 2. Fill in the names of the state capitals.

☐ 3. Fill in the major

    ☐ Oceans     ☐ Mountains

    ☐ Bays       ☐ Rivers

    ☐ Lakes     ☐ Other _____

☐ 4. List states that are north, south, east, or west of other states:

    ___north___ of ___Oregon___ ?     _____ of _____ ?

    _____ of _____ ?     _____ of _____ ?

    _____ of _____ ?     _____ of _____ ?

☐ 5. Check today's weather map in your local newspaper. Use illustrations to indicate the weather for _____ states. See the following examples:

Sunny

Cloudy

Rainy

Snowy

Copyright © 2008 by John Wiley & Sons. Inc.

**Differentiated Instruction Made Easy**

# The Fifty States Tasks *(continued)*

Stormy

Other _____

☐ 6. Pick a state you have never been to. List the states you would pass through to get there from your house.

☐ 7. Name the states that border it.

☐ 8. Pick a state you would like to visit: _____.

    ☐ Why did you choose this state?

    ☐ Check the weather map symbol and decide what to pack to take on your trip.

    ☐ Select _____ attractions to visit.

    ☐ Add _____ facts you need to know to have a successful trip.

☐ 9. Draw a map of your own state or another state. Write in:

    ☐ The capital city     ☐ Rivers

    ☐ Lakes     ☐ Attractions

    ☐ Airports     ☐ Parks

    ☐ Bordering states     ☐ Other _____

    ☐ Major cities

Copyright © 2008 by John Wiley & Sons. Inc.

# The Fifty States Tasks (continued)

☐ 10. Select a state and write or illustrate your findings on the following topics:

    ☐ Population    ☐ Products    ☐ Major industries

    ☐ Climate    ☐ Other _____

☐ 11. List all the states that border:

    ☐ An ocean    ☐ A bay    ☐ Other states only
    ☐ Another country    ☐ A large lake

☐ 12. Which states do NOT border water?

☐ 13. From memory, ☐ write ☐ tell ☐ record the names of as many of the fifty ☐ states ☐ states plus capitals as you can think of.

☐ 14. Which two states are NOT part of the mainland?

☐ 15. Which state is a series of islands?

☐ 16. Create _____ questions for your classmates about a specific state.

    Use in ☐ a classroom game    ☐ a computer game

    ☐ other _____.

Copyright © 2008 by John Wiley & Sons, Inc.

**Differentiated Instruction Made Easy**

# Outline of U.S. Map

| | | | |
|---|---|---|---|
| Alabama | Indiana | Nebraska | Rhode Island |
| Alaska | Iowa | Nevada | South Carolina |
| Arizona | Kansas | New Hampshire | South Dakota |
| Arkansas | Kentucky | New Jersey | Tennessee |
| California | Louisiana | New Mexico | Texas |
| Colorado | Maine | New York | Utah |
| Connecticut | Maryland | North Carolina | Vermont |
| Delaware | Massachusetts | North Dakota | Virginia |
| Florida | Michigan | Ohio | Washington |
| Georgia | Minnesota | Oklahoma | West Virginia |
| Hawaii | Mississippi | Oregon | Wisconsin |
| Idaho | Missouri | Pennsylvania | Wyoming |
| Illinois | Montana | | |

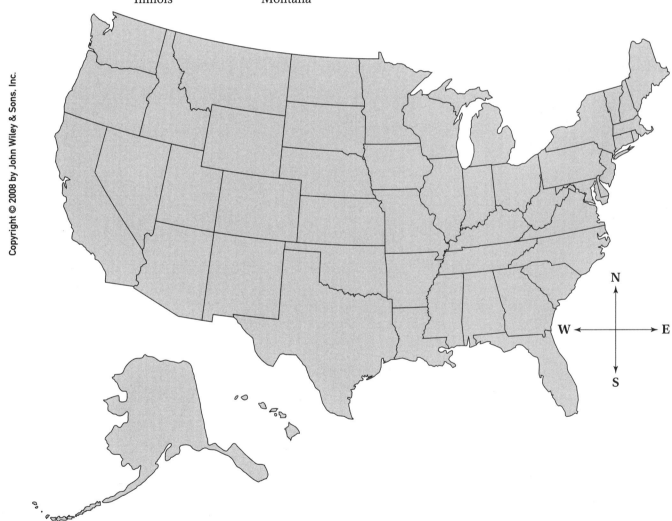

Copyright © 2008 by John Wiley & Sons. Inc.

**Geography Activities**

# Blank U.S. Map

| | | | |
|---|---|---|---|
| Alabama | Indiana | Nebraska | Rhode Island |
| Alaska | Iowa | Nevada | South Carolina |
| Arizona | Kansas | New Hampshire | South Dakota |
| Arkansas | Kentucky | New Jersey | Tennessee |
| California | Louisiana | New Mexico | Texas |
| Colorado | Maine | New York | Utah |
| Connecticut | Maryland | North Carolina | Vermont |
| Delaware | Massachusetts | North Dakota | Virginia |
| Florida | Michigan | Ohio | Washington |
| Georgia | Minnesota | Oklahoma | West Virginia |
| Hawaii | Mississippi | Oregon | Wisconsin |
| Idaho | Missouri | Pennsylvania | Wyoming |
| Illinois | Montana | | |

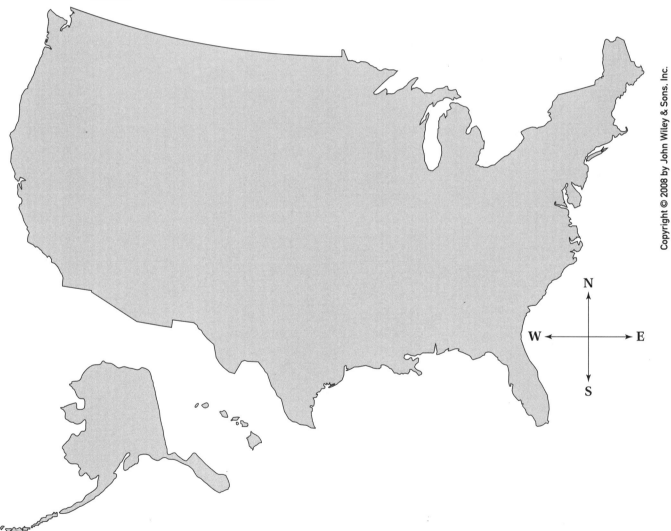

Copyright © 2008 by John Wiley & Sons, Inc.

**Differentiated Instruction Made Easy**

# Countries of the World Contract

Copyright © 2008 by John Wiley & Sons. Inc.

Country I choose to study: _____.

I am choosing this country because _____

_____.

I will choose _____ activities and complete _____

assigned activities by _____.
                              Date


_____
                 Teacher


_____
                 Student

#  Countries of the World Tasks

- ☐ 1. ☐ Write ☐ Make an audio recording ☐ Make a video recording
  ☐ Tell ☐ Draw ☐ Other _____ about the country's

  | | | |
  |---|---|---|
  | ☐ Population | ☐ Art | ☐ Animals |
  | ☐ Language | ☐ Geography | ☐ Vegetation |
  | ☐ Money system | ☐ History | ☐ Music |
  | ☐ Climate | ☐ Religion | ☐ Imports |
  | ☐ Tourist attractions | ☐ Clothing | ☐ Exports |
  | ☐ Transportation | ☐ Products | ☐ Culture |
  | ☐ Government | ☐ Famous people | ☐ Foods |
  | ☐ Sports | ☐ Landmarks | ☐ Flag |
  | ☐ Holidays | ☐ Customs | ☐ Other _____ |

- ☐ 2. Create a travel brochure to attract tourists to that country.
- ☐ 3. Collect stamps from that country.
- ☐ 4. Create an airline poster advertising that country.
- ☐ 5. Make up a restaurant menu for that country.
- ☐ 6. Collect some recipes from that country.
- ☐ 7. Make up _____ math problems using the monetary system of that country.
- ☐ 8. Find out the difference between the time in that country and the time in _____.
- ☐ 9. Plan an itinerary of your visit to that country.
- ☐ 10. Pack a bag for your trip. What will you need?
- ☐ 11. If you were in that country, what would you
  - ☐ want to see?  ☐ want to eat?
  - ☐ want to do?  ☐ want to buy?
- ☐ 12. Collect pictures about that country. Make a scrapbook.
- ☐ 13. Design _____ postcards from that country.
- ☐ 14. What would you like to share with the people of the country you chose?
- ☐ 15. Which customs of that country do you wish we had in our own country?
- ☐ 16. Interview a person from the country you chose and create a presentation for your class.

Copyright © 2008 by John Wiley & Sons, Inc.

# Transportation Worksheet

- ☐ 1. I chose this transportation card: _____

- ☐ 2. Find out the following about your transportation choice:
  - ☐ Where used      ☐ Climate for
  - ☐ History of       ☐ Care of
  - ☐ Used in work    ☐ Fuel
  - ☐ Used in play    ☐ What it's made of
  - ☐ Inventor        ☐ Advantages as transportation
  - ☐ Speed          ☐ Disadvantages as transportation
  - ☐ Efficiency

- ☐ 3. Design a new model of this form of transportation.

- ☐ 4. Construct the model out of ☐ clay ☐ papier-mâché ☐ wire ☐ soap ☐ wood ☐ other _____.

- ☐ 5. Create a mobile representing it.

- ☐ 6. Produce a TV spot advertising it.

- ☐ 7. Pretend you are a salesperson. Try to sell it to

  _____.

- ☐ 8. Using _____ of the transportation cards, group them into:
  - ☐ Land transportation
  - ☐ Air transportation
  - ☐ Water transportation

- ☐ 9. Using _____ of the transportation cards, list
  - ☐ those you have tried.
  - ☐ those you have not tried.
  - ☐ those you would like to try.

Copyright © 2008 by John Wiley & Sons, Inc.

# Transportation Cards

Copyright © 2008 by John Wiley & Sons. Inc.

**Differentiated Instruction Made Easy**

# Transportation Cards *(continued)*

Copyright © 2008 by John Wiley & Sons, Inc.

# Transportation Cards *(continued)*

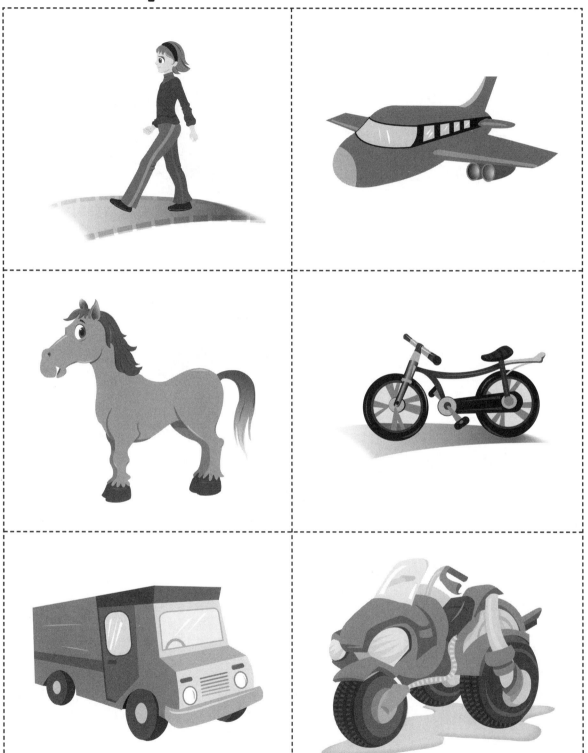

Copyright © 2008 by John Wiley & Sons, Inc.

**Differentiated Instruction Made Easy**

# Chapter 7

# Science Activities

This chapter contains activities guaranteed to light up the hearts and minds of budding scientists—and any student who needs a variety of opportunities to learn using hands-on activities. Now is the time to open your cabinets and unpack the ant farm, the aquarium, the magnets, the seeds, and all the other tools that support meaningful scientific learning opportunities.

Science has no boundaries. Reading, math, writing, and other communication skills all support science. Here, scientific exploration in multilevel forms involves wheels, contracts, and task cards. The wheels on the following pages can be combined in any number of ways to create activities geared to your students' levels and interests. Each contract offers a variety of experimental possibilities and research opportunities for any age. You can divide a contract into smaller experiments or use it as a whole for your "junior" scientists with "senior" ideas. Duplicate the task cards for use in a science center. Choose cards that relate to a particular theme, or mix and match them.

# Sensational Five Contract

I, _____, agree to use my common senses

to complete _____ tasks of my own choosing and _____

assigned tasks by _____.
                        Date

_____
              Teacher

_____
              Scientist

Copyright © 2008 by John Wiley & Sons. Inc.

# Sensational Five: Fact-Finding Activities

Use ☐ your science book ☐ an encyclopedia ☐ library resources ☐ the Internet ☐ a video ☐ newspapers and magazines to complete the following tasks:

☐ 1. Create an organizer in which to store your scientific information on the senses: ☐ Box ☐ File folder ☐ Computer file ☐ Binder

☐ Other _____.

☐ 2. In your organizer, include the following information:

☐ The names of the five senses

☐ An illustration of each sense

☐ _____ things you smell

☐ _____ things you feel using touch

☐ _____ things you taste

☐ _____ things you see

☐ _____ things you hear

☐ 3. Use your creative skills to decorate your organizer.

Copyright © 2008 by John Wiley & Sons. Inc.

**Science Activities**

# Sensational Five Tasks

Now that you have gathered this information:

☐   1. Choose _____ of your senses. ☐ Write ☐ Illustrate ☐ Tell ☐ Record ☐ Other _____ to demonstrate your knowledge about these senses.

☐   2. Cut out _____ pictures from _____ showing the senses you listed.

☐   3. Honor _____ of your senses by creating a collage that shows how you use those senses in everyday life.

☐   4. ☐ List ☐ Describe ☐ Illustrate your favorite sensations and when they are useful to you.

☐   5. Create a list of _____ nice things you can do with your sense of _____.

☐   6. Make a recording of _____ sounds you hear in the classroom in _____ minutes.

☐   7. List _____ objects you see ☐ in your desk ☐ on the teacher's desk ☐ out the window ☐ other _____.

☐   8. Imagine you're the color coordinator for your ☐ bedroom ☐ family room ☐ playroom ☐ reading corner. Which colors would you select and why? ☐ Write ☐ Illustrate ☐ Create a diorama of your space.

☐   9. ☐ Interview a deaf person and ☐ write ☐ record ☐ tell ☐ other _____ what you learn.

☐ 10. Read ☐ Watch a video about Helen Keller's life. How did she adapt without two of her senses?

☐ 11. Imagine you are blind and have a Guide Dog. ☐ Interview a blind person. ☐ Research and write ☐ Record a video about how a person who is blind uses ☐ a Guide Dog ☐ a cane ☐ other.

☐ 12. ☐ Read ☐ Watch a video about people who are born without one or more senses.

☐ 13. ☐ Read ☐ Watch a video about people who have lost one or more senses due to illness or an accident.

☐ 14. Research a disability that affects one of the five senses.

☐ 15. Interview _____ people. Find out each person's favorite sense, and _____ things they like about using that sense.

Copyright © 2008 by John Wiley & Sons. Inc.

# Sensational Five Tasks *(continued)*

☐ 16. What color is most pleasing to your eyes? ☐ Write ☐ Tell ☐ Illustrate why.

☐ 17. Name your favorite color. ☐ Find ☐ Draw _____ things that are that color.

☐ 18. What color is least appealing to your eyes? ☐ Write ☐ Tell ☐ Illustrate why.

☐ 19. Name as many textures as you can. ☐ Find ☐ Draw ☐ List _____ objects that have these textures.

☐ 20. Wear a blindfold. Take a walk with a friend and describe what you touch and experience.

☐ 21. Prepare a smell box. Put _____ things that smell very different from each other in the box. Blindfold a friend and see how many smells your friend can identify.

☐ 22. Close your eyes and visualize a place you would like to be right now. ☐ Write about ☐ Illustrate the place and how you would use _____ of your senses there.

☐ 23. How have your previous experiences helped you visualize?

☐ 24. Put _____ objects in a ☐ mystery box ☐ bag. Ask a friend to tell you what each item is after touching them.

☐ 25. Use the mystery feel box yourself. Close your eyes and feel _____ items. Describe what they feel like to you.

☐ 26. Keep a journal or diary of all the things that are useful to your sense(s) of _____ at _____ (time) each day.

☐ 27. How else can you learn about your senses? Choose another way.

Copyright © 2008 by John Wiley & Sons, Inc.

**Science Activities**

# Our Senses

The wheels on the following pages can be used separately or combined in any number of different ways, as well as with other tools such as a multilevel gameboard or in a language development activity. They can be used by individuals or groups, and in activity centers.

Use the sample wheel on page 87 to create activities geared to the children's levels and interests. For younger children, for instance, you could prepare a wheel with pictures of a nose, eye, hand, ear, and mouth, and a spinner on top. The children could name something they can smell, for example; or find something, draw something, or write about something or. . . .

For older students, two wheels of different sizes can be combined with a spinner to produce, for instance, "Name something you can taste *and* hear" or "Name something you can smell *and* feel."

A medium-sized color wheel could be prepared and placed over a large sense wheel to produce, for example, "Name something red that you can taste" (such as an apple) or "Draw something silver that you can hear" (such as a bell). Students could color in a wheel on which you have printed the names of the colors or the names of objects that are those colors. Other choices resulting from combining two wheels could include "Name something hot that you can smell" (such as a turkey cooking) or "something rough that you can hear" (such as sandpaper on wood), and of course there will probably be some little sensualists who would like to combine *three* categories: "Name something little and purple that you can taste" (a grape).

The following pages will get you started. We have created large, medium, and small wheels to facilitate many possible combinations, such as the following example:

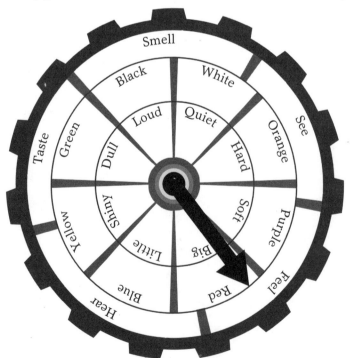

**Differentiated Instruction Made Easy**

# Our Senses Wheels

*Note to teacher:* Wheels may be enlarged as appropriate to the grade level.

Copyright © 2008 by John Wiley & Sons. Inc.

# Our Senses Wheels *(continued)*

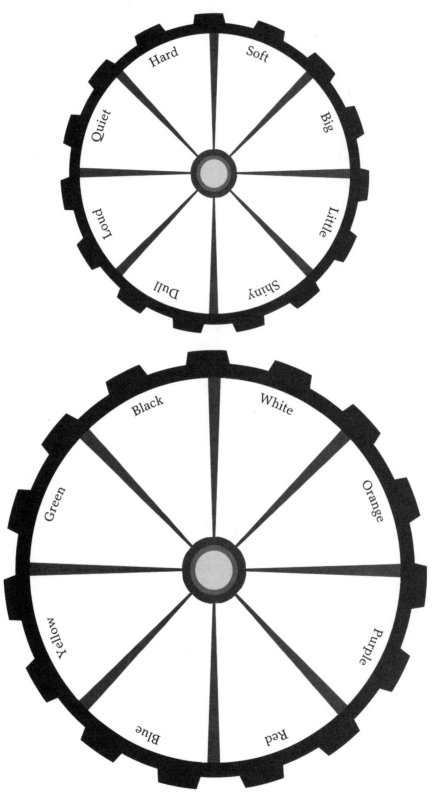

*Note to teacher:* Wheels may be enlarged as appropriate to the grade level.

Copyright © 2008 by John Wiley & Sons. Inc.

**Differentiated Instruction Made Easy**

# Insect Task Cards

The bee country of Hiveville has a new queen: Her Royal Highness Queen Bea. You are ☐ the old queen ☐ a bee worker ☐ a flower. Show Queen Bea around her new kingdom. ☐ Write ☐ Draw ☐ Record a tour around the kingdom. Use _____ to get the information you need.

Imagine you are the mayor of Bug City. ☐ List ☐ Draw ☐ Write about _____ different bugs you have in the city. Use ☐ the library ☐ magazines ☐ the school yard to find _____ kinds of bugs in Bug City. ☐ Write about ☐ Tell about kinds of bugs that would be ☐ good ☐ bad for Bug City.

Make up a comic strip about bugs. Check out your ☐ library ☐ school yard ☐ park ☐ backyard for _____ different kinds of bugs to use in the comic strip. Include some of the ☐ funny ☐ sad ☐ happy ☐ silly ☐ scary things that might happen to your bugs.

You are the ☐ teacher ☐ scientist ☐ collector. It is your ☐ job ☐ hobby ☐ assignment to find out about _____ kinds of bugs. Use your ☐ library ☐ school yard ☐ backyard ☐ park to ☐ read about ☐ observe ☐ collect insects. ☐ Draw ☐ Write about ☐ Tell about ☐ List the ☐ body parts ☐ environment ☐ habits of the insects.

BUG SAFARI! Organize a safari to hunt down bugs. Collect ☐ jars ☐ vials ☐ nets ☐ boxes for your hunt. Find _____ safari members to hunt with you. Label your bug specimen containers with
   ☐ Names of bugs     ☐ Date of find
   ☐ Location of find    ☐ Safari member who found specimen
Remember: Return bugs to the environment!

Copyright © 2008 by John Wiley & Sons, Inc.

# Reptile Contract

☐ Dinosaurs ☐ Crocodiles ☐ Snakes ☐ Turtles ☐ Lizards

☐ Other _____

Choose a reptile family from those just listed and write its name

here: _____

☐ Write ☐ Make an audio recording ☐ Make a video recording
☐ Tell ☐ Illustrate


I, _____, agree to complete

this contract by _____.

                   Date



_____

Teacher


_____

Student

Copyright © 2008 by John Wiley & Sons. Inc.

# Reptile Tasks

☐ 1. Name as many different kinds of reptiles as you can find in the reptile family you have chosen.

☐ 2. Describe _____ of the varieties in your reptile family.

☐ 3. Draw a picture of _____ kinds.

☐ 4. Describe the reptile family's:

    ☐ Habitat      ☐ Habits      ☐ Food

    ☐ Predators      ☐ Body types      ☐ Friends

    ☐ Babies and young      ☐ Life span      ☐ Other _____

☐ 5. Prepare a ☐ lecture ☐ written report ☐ poster ☐ video recording

    ☐ audio recording ☐ Web site ☐ other _____

    about the reptile family you have chosen.

☐ 6. See how much information you can find

    ☐ In an encyclopedia    ☐ In the park    ☐ In a library book

    ☐ In the yard    ☐ At the zoo    ☐ At a museum

    ☐ Online    ☐ Other _____

☐ 7. Make a list of

    ☐ Which ones are extinct

    ☐ Which ones are alive today

☐ 8. List _____ ways in which this creature is helpful.

☐ 9. List _____ ways in which this creature is harmful.

☐ 10. Make a ☐ clay ☐ papier-mâché ☐ wire ☐ other _____ model of this kind of reptile.

☐ 11. Make a reptile mobile.

☐ 12. Would you like one for a pet?

    ☐ Which one?

    ☐ Why?

    ☐ Why not?

☐ 13. Pretend you are one of these reptiles.

    ☐ What do you think about humans?

    ☐ What do you think about other animals?

    ☐ What do you think about other reptiles?

☐ 14. Create an imaginary reptile.

Copyright © 2008 by John Wiley & Sons, Inc.

**Science Activities**

# Bird Contract

- ☐ Ostrich
- ☐ Hummingbird
- ☐ Penguin
- ☐ Cuckoo
- ☐ Loon
- ☐ Pigeon
- ☐ Owl
- ☐ Hawk
- ☐ Mockingbird

- ☐ Parrot
- ☐ Parakeet
- ☐ Gull
- ☐ Tern
- ☐ Peacock
- ☐ Stork
- ☐ Woodpecker
- ☐ Canary
- ☐ Sandpiper

- ☐ Plover
- ☐ Robin
- ☐ Lark
- ☐ Sparrow
- ☐ Cardinal
- ☐ Finch
- ☐ Flamingo
- ☐ Duck
- ☐ Other _____

From the preceding list, choose a type of bird you would like to learn about: _____.

I, _____, agree to complete this

flighty contract by _____.
                           Date

_____
              Teacher

_____
              Student

Copyright © 2008 by John Wiley & Sons, Inc.

# Bird Tasks

- ☐ 1. Name as many different birds of this type as you can find in the _____.
- ☐ 2. Describe _____ kinds you have found.
- ☐ 3. ☐ Draw ☐ Find a picture or pictures of _____.
- ☐ 4. Describe:

  ☐ Habitat      ☐ Friends      ☐ Communication
  ☐ Habits      ☐ Food      ☐ Predators
  ☐ Other _____

- ☐ 5. Describe ☐ size ☐ plumage ☐ migration patterns.
- ☐ 6. Tell about nesting habits: ☐ materials ☐ location

  ☐ other _____
- ☐ 7. Find _____ pictures in _____. Cut them out, label them, and put them ☐ in a scrapbook ☐ on a bulletin board

  ☐ on a window ☐ on a poster ☐ other _____.
- ☐ 8. Describe the eggs of this kind of bird.
- ☐ 9. Find the scientific name for your bird.
- ☐ 10. Prepare ☐ a video recording ☐ an audio recording ☐ a written

  report ☐ a lecture for _____ about this family of birds.
- ☐ 11. Do a bulletin board about the birds with _____

  classmates.
- ☐ 12. Make a bird mobile.
- ☐ 13. Make a mural with _____ showing different

  varieties of this bird family.
- ☐ 14. Make a ☐ clay ☐ papier-mâché ☐ soap ☐ wire

  ☐ other _____ model of this kind of bird.
- ☐ 15. Pretend that you are this kind of bird. ☐ Tell ☐ Write
  ☐ Illustrate ☐ Record
    ☐ What makes you feel safe
    ☐ What makes you feel happy
    ☐ What makes you afraid
    ☐ What makes you sad
- ☐ 16. Map the migration patterns of your bird.
- ☐ 17. Research community resources for sick or injured birds.
- ☐ 18. Create a list of endangered birds. ☐ Graph ☐ Describe in your own way the current populations.
- ☐ 19. Select your own bird activity.

Copyright © 2008 by John Wiley & Sons, Inc.

**Science Activities**

# Task Cards for Serious Bird Students

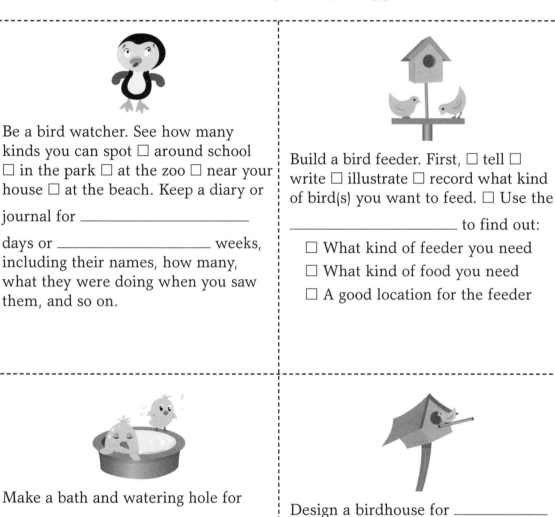

Be a bird watcher. See how many kinds you can spot ☐ around school ☐ in the park ☐ at the zoo ☐ near your house ☐ at the beach. Keep a diary or journal for _____ days or _____ weeks, including their names, how many, what they were doing when you saw them, and so on.

Build a bird feeder. First, ☐ tell ☐ write ☐ illustrate ☐ record what kind of bird(s) you want to feed. ☐ Use the _____ to find out:
☐ What kind of feeder you need
☐ What kind of food you need
☐ A good location for the feeder

Make a bath and watering hole for birds. Use your _____ to check what would be a good, safe location.

Design a birdhouse for _____ [name of bird]. Use the _____ to:
☐ Find out what type of house to build.
☐ List which materials you will need.
☐ Build it ☐ alone ☐ with _____.

Copyright © 2008 by John Wiley & Sons. Inc.

**Differentiated Instruction Made Easy**

# Task Cards for Serious
# Bird Students *(continued)*

Copyright © 2008 by John Wiley & Sons, Inc.

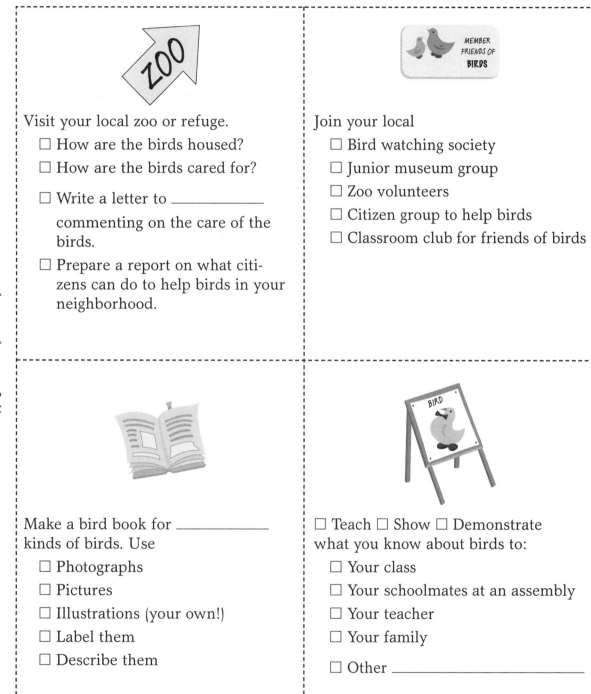

Visit your local zoo or refuge.
- ☐ How are the birds housed?
- ☐ How are the birds cared for?

- ☐ Write a letter to _____ commenting on the care of the birds.
- ☐ Prepare a report on what citizens can do to help birds in your neighborhood.

Join your local
- ☐ Bird watching society
- ☐ Junior museum group
- ☐ Zoo volunteers
- ☐ Citizen group to help birds
- ☐ Classroom club for friends of birds

Make a bird book for _____ kinds of birds. Use
- ☐ Photographs
- ☐ Pictures
- ☐ Illustrations (your own!)
- ☐ Label them
- ☐ Describe them

☐ Teach ☐ Show ☐ Demonstrate what you know about birds to:
- ☐ Your class
- ☐ Your schoolmates at an assembly
- ☐ Your teacher
- ☐ Your family
- ☐ Other _____

**Science Activities**

# Animal Contract

Copyright © 2008 by John Wiley & Sons. Inc.

☐ Dogs ☐ Cats ☐ Bears ☐ Horses ☐ Cows ☐ Other _____

Choose an animal family from the preceding list: _____

I, _____, agree to complete

this contract by _____.
                    Date


_____
            Witness


_____
            Teacher

# Animal Tasks

☐ 1. Name as many different kinds of animals as you can find in the animal family you have chosen.

☐ 2. Describe _____ varieties in your animal family.

☐ 3. Draw a picture of _____ kinds.

☐ 4. Describe:

☐ Habitat ☐ Habits ☐ Food
☐ Predators ☐ Body types ☐ Friends
☐ Babies/young ☐ Life span ☐ Other _____

☐ 5. Prepare ☐ a lecture ☐ a written report ☐ a poster ☐ a video recording ☐ a show ☐ an audio recording ☐ a Web site ☐ other _____ about the animal family you have chosen.

☐ 6. See how much information you can find

☐ In an encyclopedia ☐ In the park ☐ In a library book
☐ In the yard ☐ At the zoo ☐ At a museum
☐ Online ☐ Other _____

☐ 7. Make a list of

☐ Which ones are extinct

☐ Which ones are alive today

☐ 8. List _____ ways in which this animal is helpful.

☐ 9. List _____ ways in which this animal is harmful.

Copyright © 2008 by John Wiley & Sons, Inc.

**Science Activities**

# Animal Tasks *(continued)*

☐ 10. Make a ☐ clay ☐ papier-mâché ☐ wire ☐ other _____ model of this kind of animal.

☐ 11. Make an animal mobile.

☐ 12. Would you like one for a pet?

    ☐ Which one?

    ☐ Why?

    ☐ Why not?

☐ 13. Pretend you are one of these animals.

    ☐ What do you think about humans?

    ☐ What do you think about other animals?

    ☐ What do you think about reptiles?

☐ 14. Research community resources for sick or injured animals.

☐ 15. Create a list of endangered animals. ☐ Graph ☐ Describe in your own way the current populations.

☐ 16. Design a fantasy animal.

Copyright © 2008 by John Wiley & Sons. Inc.

**Differentiated Instruction Made Easy**

# Animal Task Cards

Copyright © 2008 by John Wiley & Sons, Inc.

## ANIMAL CARE!!

Pretend you are a new pet owner.

☐ Write ☐ Tell ☐ Create a video or DVD about
   ☐ How to keep your pet healthy.
   ☐ What to do if your pet becomes sick or injured.
   ☐ What the average life span is for your pet.
☐ Other _____

## ANIMAL FOR A DAY!

☐ Create an ☐ animal costume ☐ puppet.
☐ Make up an animal language.
☐ Create a recipe for your animal's favorite food.
☐ Design an animal home.
☐ Create animal family members and friends.

# Animal Task Cards *(continued)*

## ANIMAL FEELINGS!

☐ Write ☐ Tell ☐ Record a video or DVD about

    ☐ Which animal you would be.

    ☐ Your worst experience.

    ☐ Your best experience.

    ☐ What you are most proud of.

    ☐ Who your best friends are and why.

## MAKE YOUR OWN ANIMAL BOOK!

Write and illustrate a storybook about your favorite animal. Describe and illustrate

    ☐ What happens at the beginning of your story.

    ☐ What happens in the middle of your story.

Read your book to your ☐ friend ☐ class ☐ teacher ☐ family.

Copyright © 2008 by John Wiley & Sons. Inc.

**Differentiated Instruction Made Easy**

# Fish and Water Mammals Contract

☐ Aquarium fish      ☐ Saltwater fish

☐ Freshwater fish     ☐ Whales

☐ Dolphins          ☐ Other _____

From the preceding list, choose a type of water species you would like to learn about: _____.

I, _____, agree to complete this contract

by _____.

     Date

_____

Teacher

_____

Student

Copyright © 2008 by John Wiley & Sons, Inc.

**Science Activities**                           **101**

# Fish and Water Mammals Tasks

☐ 1. Using ☐ the Internet ☐ encyclopedia ☐ the library ☐ other

_____, name as many different kinds of ☐ fish

☐ water mammals of this type as you can find.

☐ 2. Describe _____ kinds you have found.

☐ 3. ☐ Draw ☐ Find pictures of _____.

☐ 4. Describe:

☐ Habitat      ☐ Friends            ☐ Communication

☐ Habits       ☐ Eating habits      ☐ Predators

☐ Size         ☐ Migration patterns ☐ Other _____

☐ 5. Find _____ pictures in _____.

Cut out and put ☐ in a scrapbook ☐ on a bulletin board ☐ on

a window ☐ on a poster ☐ other _____. Label

each picture.

☐ 6. Find the scientific names for _____ fish

in _____.

☐ 7. Prepare ☐ a video recording ☐ an audio recording ☐ a written

report ☐ a lecture for ☐ a friend ☐ the whole class about this

species.

☐ 8. Create a bulletin board about this species ☐ by yourself ☐ with

classmates.

☐ 9. Create a ☐ mobile ☐ diorama of this species.

☐ 10. Draw a mural showing different varieties of this species.

☐ 11. Make a ☐ clay ☐ papier-mâché ☐ soap ☐ wire ☐ other

_____ model of this species.

☐ 12. Pretend you are this species. ☐ Tell ☐ Write ☐ Illustrate
☐ Record

☐ What makes you feel safe

☐ What makes you feel happy

☐ What makes you afraid

☐ What makes you sad

Copyright © 2008 by John Wiley & Sons. Inc.

# Fish and Water Mammals
## Tasks *(continued)*

☐ 13. Map the migration patterns of this species.

☐ 14. Research community resources for sick or injured water species.

☐ 15. Create a list of endangered fish or other water species. ☐ Graph ☐ Describe in your own way the current populations.

Copyright © 2008 by John Wiley & Sons, Inc.

# Chapter 8

# Media Activities

This chapter is designed to enable learners to use the newspaper and other communication media as motivational learning tools that incorporate all elements of the curriculum. Newspapers, magazines, computers, and journals should be readily available in the classroom. The tasks offered here fit easily into a learning-center model with small groups of students, as part of a whole-class activity, or as activities for individual students to support their special interests.

These tasks are not limited to newspaper activities. Many of them can teach the understanding and use of store catalogs, television news, consumer research on the Internet, and many other resources.

# Newsworthy Activity Contract

I, _____, hereby agree to act

as special reporter on _____

assignments of my choice plus _____ assigned tasks. I realize

that my deadline is _____.
                       Date

_____
            Student

_____
            Teacher

Copyright © 2008 by John Wiley & Sons. Inc.

# News Assignments

☐   1. ☐ List ☐ Cut out and paste up ☐ Count ☐ Other _____ all the stories you find in the newspaper about a topic of your choice.

☐   2. Choose an article from _____ and illustrate the story.

☐   3. Write ☐ Make an audio recording ☐ Make a video recording ☐ Report to the class a summary of ☐ the feature story ☐ the weather report ☐ a news story ☐ a sports story ☐ other _____.

☐   4. Design an advertisement about ☐ an event ☐ a product ☐ an adventure ☐ other _____.

☐   5. Count and chart the various kinds of stories in the newspaper. Do this for _____ days. Present a summary of your results to the class.

☐   6. Create your own comic strip.

☐   7. ☐ Write ☐ Record ☐ Illustrate your own special-interest story.

☐   8. Pick a current event you are concerned about and ☐ write ☐ make a video recording ☐ make an audio recording of an editorial.

☐   9. Make a scrapbook and paste in examples of different sections of the newspaper.

☐ 10. Find _____ interviews about ☐ an athlete ☐ a politician ☐ an actor ☐ a musician ☐ a humanitarian ☐ other _____. Cut out and create a who's who encyclopedia.

☐ 11. Interview ☐ a friend ☐ a teacher ☐ the principal ☐ an aide ☐ a neighbor ☐ the custodian ☐ a police officer ☐ a senior citizen ☐ the cook ☐ a store owner ☐ a relative ☐ other _____. ☐ Write ☐ Make a video recording ☐ Make an audio recording ☐ Tell about this special person.

☐ 12. Look in the classified ads section of the newspaper and find _____ ads that interest you. Cut them out and ☐ tell someone why you chose them ☐ write down the reasons they interest you ☐ put them in a scrapbook.

☐ 13. Choose events that you would like to attend after looking at advertisements in the newspaper. Make a calendar and plan your ☐ day ☐ week ☐ month of dream adventures.

Copyright © 2008 by John Wiley & Sons. Inc.

# News Assignments *(continued)*

☐ 14. Write a letter to the editor of your newspaper.

☐ 15. Write an advice column for your classroom. Have _____ of your classmates ☐ write ☐ tell you their problems. ☐ Write ☐ Tell ☐ Record your sensible, super solutions.

☐ 16. Pick a topic from the front page of the newspaper. Follow the story daily. Keep a notebook or scrapbook. Present an update to your class every _____ days.

☐ 17. ☐ Write ☐ Record a movie review or a review of some other exciting event you have attended.

☐ 18. Act out one of the scenes from the funnies with _____ friends. Costumes are welcome!

☐ 19. Pick a headline without reading the story. ☐ Write ☐ Make an audio recording ☐ Make a video recording ☐ Illustrate what you think the article is about. ☐ Read ☐ Have someone read to you the article and see how close you were to the actual story.

☐ 20. You may watch television for only _____ minutes per day. Carefully choose your favorite programs and make a TV calendar for _____ days.

☐ 21. Make a weather calendar. Write down your own predictions. Then using ☐ TV ☐ the newspaper ☐ the Internet, forecast the weather report and write down those predictions for _____ days. See who does better—you or your weatherperson!

☐ 22. Cut out _____ ads from a ☐ newspaper ☐ magazine. Make a scrapbook with two sections—believable and unbelievable—and ☐ write ☐ tell your reasons.

☐ 23. Using the ☐ newspaper ☐ TV ☐ Internet ☐ other _____, create _____ of your own newsworthy tasks.

Copyright © 2008 by John Wiley & Sons. Inc.

# News Wheels

*Note to teacher:* Wheels may be enlarged as appropriate to the grade level.

Copyright © 2008 by John Wiley & Sons, Inc.

# News Wheels *(continued)*

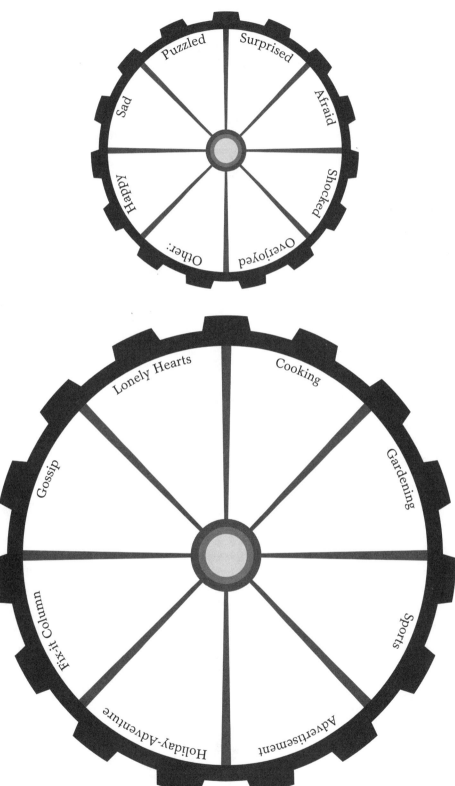

*Note to teacher:* Wheels may be enlarged as appropriate to the grade level.

Copyright © 2008 by John Wiley & Sons. Inc.

# News Wheels *(continued)*

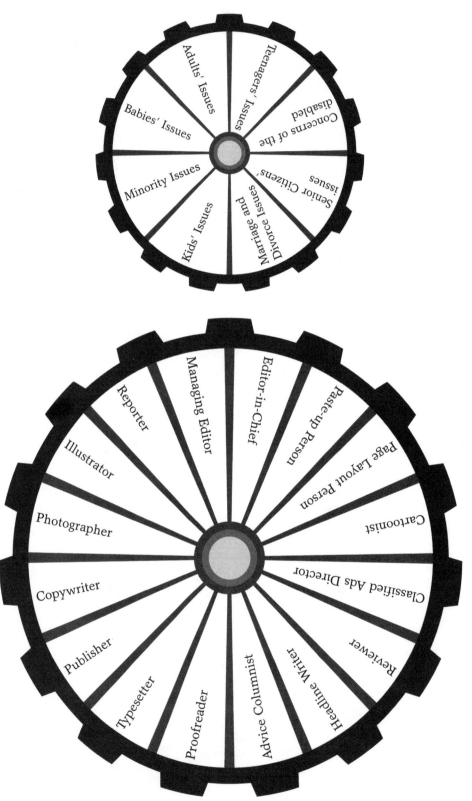

*Note to teacher:* Wheels may be enlarged as appropriate to the grade level.

**Differentiated Instruction Made Easy**

Copyright © 2008 by John Wiley & Sons, Inc.

# News Task Cards

| | | |
|---|---|---|
| Illustrate | Videotape | Write about |
| Act out | Use the Internet | Make a scrapbook |
| Create _____ of your own tasks | Read _____ articles about _____ | Help a pal learn about _____ |

Copyright © 2008 by John Wiley & Sons, Inc.

# News Task Cards *(continued)*

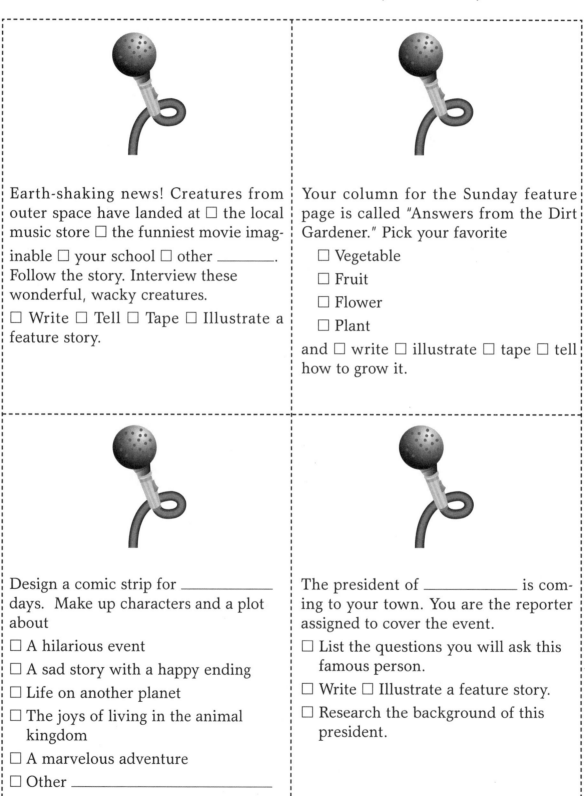

Earth-shaking news! Creatures from outer space have landed at ☐ the local music store ☐ the funniest movie imaginable ☐ your school ☐ other _____. Follow the story. Interview these wonderful, wacky creatures.

☐ Write ☐ Tell ☐ Tape ☐ Illustrate a feature story.

---

Your column for the Sunday feature page is called "Answers from the Dirt Gardener." Pick your favorite

  ☐ Vegetable

  ☐ Fruit

  ☐ Flower

  ☐ Plant

and ☐ write ☐ illustrate ☐ tape ☐ tell how to grow it.

---

Design a comic strip for _____ days. Make up characters and a plot about

☐ A hilarious event

☐ A sad story with a happy ending

☐ Life on another planet

☐ The joys of living in the animal kingdom

☐ A marvelous adventure

☐ Other _____

---

The president of _____ is coming to your town. You are the reporter assigned to cover the event.

☐ List the questions you will ask this famous person.

☐ Write ☐ Illustrate a feature story.

☐ Research the background of this president.

Copyright © 2008 by John Wiley & Sons. Inc.

# News Task Cards *(continued)*

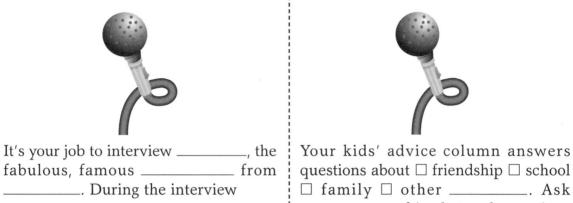

It's your job to interview _____, the fabulous, famous _____ from _____. During the interview

- ☐ A strong wind blows off this person's wig
- ☐ This person's pet rattlesnake bites your leg
- ☐ You discover this person is a fake and not the real thing
- ☐ This person vanishes before your eyes

☐ Tell ☐ Write ☐ Illustrate
☐ Cartoon ☐ Act out the interview.

Your kids' advice column answers questions about ☐ friendship ☐ school ☐ family ☐ other _____. Ask _____ friends to ask questions and

- ☐ Write
- ☐ Act out
- ☐ Illustrate
- ☐ Cartoon
- ☐ Tape your extravagant answers and silly solutions

Copyright © 2008 by John Wiley & Sons. Inc.

# Application for Media Job

Job applied for: _____

Name: _____
                     First                        Last

School now attending: _____

School address: _____
                       Number                Street

How I found out about the job: _____

Qualifications the job requires: _____

How I can meet these qualifications: _____

_____

Why I want the job: _____

_____

Who I know in this line of work: _____

_____

I hereby certify that all of the above information is true and correct.

_____       _____

Signature of Applicant                 Date

For teacher use only:

This application was processed and the above applicant selected to receive the

job on _____ day of _____, 20_____.

_____

Teacher

Copyright © 2008 by John Wiley & Sons, Inc.

**Differentiated Instruction Made Easy**

# You Name It! Newspaper Worksheet

_____ HIRED AS ★ REPORTER

Today is _____, _____, _____
            Day              Month              Year

(Place a drawing or photo of YOU here!)

## Feature Story
## WONDERFUL! WONDERFUL!

_____ has been chosen to be Star
(Your name)

Reporter. The editor assigns _____ tasks. The Star

Reporter can choose _____ tasks to be completed

by _____.
                        Date

☐ WRITE     ☐ ACT OUT     ☐ DRAW     ☐ TAPE     ☐ TELL
about:

☐ An invention
☐ A peace plan
☐ A smashing discovery
☐ Transportation
☐ A super, joy-filled event
☐ A heartbreaking disaster
☐ A famous person
☐ A concern of people your age
☐ Local     ☐ State     ☐ National
government

☐ An editorial about a concern you have
☐ An evaluation of a Web site
☐ A review of a play, movie, concert
☐ A special recipe
☐ A how-to-make-it article
☐ News flash
☐ A book review
☐ Other _____

Copyright © 2008 by John Wiley & Sons. Inc.

**Media Activities**

# Chapter 9

# Art Activities

There is an art to teaching art so that students will develop their true and natural abilities. Many of us grew up taking art classes in which everyone did the same thing in the same way. On the surface it seems easier and less time consuming to have whole classes working on the same project, but is it really? Can't art classes in which students work on individual projects be easy to teach, and much more fun? And once a variety of materials are available, won't preparation and instruction be less time-consuming for the teacher?

Honoring individual choices will surely take us a long way toward enabling students to develop their own creative styles. Other Michelangelos, Rodins, and Warhols are just waiting to be given a chance. This is an opportunity to encourage the development of any child's inner artist.

This chapter includes an art contract that covers many media choices and a myriad of ways to start individual artistic endeavors. As with each of our contracts, there is a place for you to add your ideas and a place for your students to add their own idea for projects. Won't it be fun to ignite the sparks and watch your students create?

# Art Contract

Copyright © 2008 by John Wiley & Sons, Inc.

I, _____, want to create a unique and special piece
of art. I will select a project from the following list. The materials I will need are
_____.

   I expect to complete my project by _____, but I may request an
                                                     Date
extension at any time.


_____
   Artist's Signature


_____
   Teacher's Signature

# Art Directions

☐ 1. Select project: _____
     (such as Art Card or Wheel Activity).

☐ 2. Choose your materials.

☐ 3. Create your project.

Copyright © 2008 by John Wiley & Sons, Inc.

# Art Projects

☐  1. Create a ☐ painting ☐ sculpture ☐ collage ☐ other _____.

☐  2. Make a _____ using torn paper.

☐  3. _____ a _____ of yourself.

☐  4. Pick _____ friends. Create a mural together.

☐  5. Choose a ☐ story ☐ poem ☐ song and illustrate it.

☐  6. Design and make a puppet.

☐  7. Design and make a mask.

☐  8. Become a fashion designer. Design _____.

☐  9. Create a _____ of your ☐ pet ☐ friend ☐ family member ☐ other _____.

☐ 10. Make a present for _____.

☐ 11. Make a decoration for ☐ a holiday ☐ a party ☐ a festival ☐ other _____ for ☐ your home ☐ a senior center.

☐ 12. Create a shadowbox of _____.

☐ 13. Create a mosaic using materials from ☐ the school yard ☐ your home ☐ a park ☐ other _____.

☐ 14. Make a _____ about
    ☐ An event in your life
    ☐ A dream you had
    ☐ A dream for the future
    ☐ A fantasy world
    ☐ A new animal
    ☐ A monster
    ☐ A creature from outer space
    ☐ An article of clothing
    ☐ A type of vehicle
    ☐ Other _____

Copyright © 2008 by John Wiley & Sons, Inc.

# Art Projects *(continued)*

☐ 15. Use the computer. Create a _____.

☐ 16. Create an ad for _____. Use ☐ the computer ☐ art supplies ☐ other _____.

☐ 17. Design _____ greeting cards.

☐ 18. Create a _____ for the bulletin board.

☐ 19. Create a poster for _____.

☐ 20. Now that you have decided which supplies you want to use, add _____ supplies that you haven't used before.

☐ 21. Now that you have created your project, teach it to ☐ a friend ☐ relatives ☐ a senior citizen.

☐ 22. Create your own masterpiece.

☐ 23. Create a color wheel.

☐ 24. Create a palette by mixing your own colors.

☐ 25. Teach _____ how to clean and organize art materials.

Copyright © 2008 by John Wiley & Sons. Inc.

# Suggested Art Center Supplies

- ☐ Finger paints
- ☐ Poster paints
- ☐ Tempera paints
- ☐ Watercolors
- ☐ Colored pencils
- ☐ Colored chalk
- ☐ Pastels
- ☐ Charcoal
- ☐ Crayons
- ☐ Calligraphy pens
- ☐ Inks
- ☐ Food coloring
- ☐ Paper
- ☐ Glue
- ☐ Rubber cement
- ☐ Starch
- ☐ Flour
- ☐ Paintbrushes
- ☐ Ruler
- ☐ Compass
- ☐ Spatula
- ☐ Scissors
- ☐ Eraser(s)
- ☐ Stapler
- ☐ Paper clips
- ☐ Paper towels
- ☐ Tracing paper
- ☐ Graph paper
- ☐ Computer
- ☐ Camera

- ☐ Egg cartons
- ☐ Grocery meat trays
- ☐ Boxes
- ☐ Tubes
- ☐ Milk cartons
- ☐ Soap flakes
- ☐ Bars of soap
- ☐ Magazines
- ☐ Newspapers
- ☐ Old greeting cards
- ☐ Wrapping paper
- ☐ Tissue paper
- ☐ Brown paper
- ☐ Butcher paper
- ☐ Waxed paper
- ☐ Wallpaper
- ☐ Glitter
- ☐ Stickers
- ☐ Rickrack
- ☐ Yarn
- ☐ String
- ☐ Wire
- ☐ Noodles
- ☐ Beans
- ☐ Nuts
- ☐ Seeds
- ☐ Wood
- ☐ Cotton balls
- ☐ Wire
- ☐ Film

- ☐ Video
- ☐ Feathers
- ☐ Fabrics
- ☐ Beads
- ☐ Nuts and bolts
- ☐ Sand
- ☐ Dirt
- ☐ Pebbles
- ☐ Stones
- ☐ Eggshells
- ☐ Salt
- ☐ Ice cream sticks
- ☐ Tongue depressors
- ☐ Toothpicks
- ☐ Twigs
- ☐ Shells
- ☐ Paper cups
- ☐ Paper plates
- ☐ Styrofoam
- ☐ Straws
- ☐ Clay
- ☐ Play dough
- ☐ Cans
- ☐ Foil
- ☐ Sponges
- ☐ Stamps
- ☐ Toothbrushes
- ☐ Screening
- ☐ Feathers

☐ Other _____

☐ Other _____

☐ Other _____

Copyright © 2008 by John Wiley & Sons, Inc.

# Art Idea Cards

Create something about one of your dreams.

Create something to music.

Create something for the future.

Create your own wallpaper.

Create something that could not be real.

Create something to make someone happy.

Create something to give to _____.

Create something that is a design.

Create something good enough to _____.

Copyright © 2008 by John Wiley & Sons. Inc.

**Differentiated Instruction Made Easy**

# Art Idea Cards *(continued)*

Create something to decorate your _____.

Create something to hang on the wall.

Create something to hang from the ceiling.

Create something you and your friend can play with.

Create something the whole class can enjoy.

Create something to give to your pet.

Create something for the holiday.

Create something funny.

Create something to tell about your favorite _____.

Copyright © 2008 by John Wiley & Sons, Inc.

# Art Idea Cards *(continued)*

Create something absolutely impossible.

Create something you can wear.

Create something about an event in your life.

Create something that tells who you are.

Create something about a place you would like to visit.

Create something for your family.

Copyright © 2008 by John Wiley & Sons. Inc.

**Differentiated Instruction Made Easy**

# Art History Task Cards and Wheel

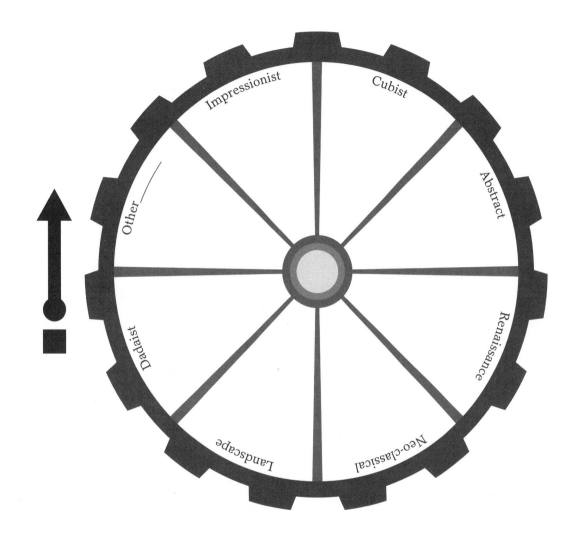

Copyright © 2008 by John Wiley & Sons. Inc.

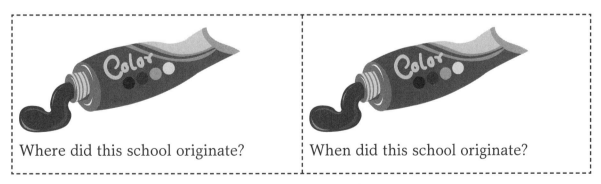

Where did this school originate? | When did this school originate?

*Note to teacher:* Wheels may be enlarged as appropriate to the grade level.

# Art History Task Cards and Wheel *(continued)*

Why did this school originate?

Name _____ artists associated with the school.

Name _____ paintings from this school and describe them.

How does this type of art make you feel?

Where can you go in your community to see this type of art?

☐ Name the places.

☐ Take a field trip to one of these places.

☐ Do a report on the art you saw.

Do a _____ in the style of this school of art.

Copyright © 2008 by John Wiley & Sons, Inc.

**Differentiated Instruction Made Easy**

# Famous Artists

Copyright © 2008 by John Wiley & Sons, Inc.

I, _____, am interested in learning about the

famous artist named _____.

I agree to complete _____ activities by _____.
                                                          Date

_____
Artistic Researcher

_____
Teacher

# Famous Artists Tasks

☐ 1. What type of art is this person associated with?

☐ 2. In what period of history did this artist work?

☐ 3. What or who were the major influences on this artist?

☐ 4. Where can you go to see some of this artist's work?

☐ 5. Name _____ famous works by this person.

☐ 6. What influence did this person have on other artists?

☐ 7. What do you ☐ like ☐ dislike about this artist's work?

☐ 8. Choose a work by this artist. Do your own version of this piece of art using your own style.

☐ 9. My favorite painting by _____

is _____

because _____.

☐ 10. If I were a famous artist I would like to _____

_____.

Copyright © 2008 by John Wiley & Sons. Inc.

# Beading and Jewelry Contract

I, _____, will do my best to have fun while completing my contract. I promise to do my best and be creative while working on each task. I will complete _____ tasks of my choice and _____ tasks chosen by my teacher. I will complete my tasks by _____.

Date

_____
Student

_____
Teacher

Copyright © 2008 by John Wiley & Sons, Inc.

# Beading and Jewelry Tasks

☐  1. Research how beads are used in different cultures using ☐ books ☐ the Internet ☐ other _____. Then write _____ sentence(s) that describe the culture and how they use beads. Draw a picture of the beads.

☐  2. Create a ☐ bracelet ☐ dream catcher ☐ belt ☐ key chain ☐ bookmark.

☐  3. Create an object with beads made from ☐ 1 ☐ 2 ☐ 3 colors of ☐ baking clay ☐ wood ☐ papier-mâche ☐ other _____. With both hands roll the clay into three balls. Roll the balls of clay into snakes and cut into small beads. Pierce the beads with a toothpick and string them.

☐  4. Describe to a ☐ friend ☐ teacher ☐ parent ☐ other _____ how to make a bracelet. What types of materials do you need? Write ☐ _____ sentence(s) ☐ _____ paragraph(s) ☐ _____ page(s). Include _____ of the following vocabulary words in your description:

|  |  |  |
|---|---|---|
| String | Crimp beads | Needle-nose pliers |
| Needles | Loop-and-toggle clasp | Bead board |
| Beads | Lobster claw clasp | Scissors |

☐  5. Using a bag of mixed beads, categorize the beads by ☐ color ☐ size ☐ shape ☐ other _____. ☐ Graph ☐ Verbalize ☐ Record the results.

☐  6. Use a bag of mixed beads to spell your name. Then
☐  Trace and color in.
☐  Record how many beads you used ☐ in each letter ☐ in your whole name.

☐  7. Create a story about a(n) ☐ bracelet ☐ necklace ☐ ring ☐ earring ☐ other _____. Illustrate ☐ character(s) ☐ event(s) ☐ setting(s).

☐  8. Make a shaker and write a song. Cut out the bottom of a paper cup. Place tinfoil over each opening. Put different kinds of beads or dried beans inside. Shake it around and have fun!

Copyright © 2008 by John Wiley & Sons, Inc.

# Beading and Jewelry
## Tasks *(continued)*

☐   9. Use ☐ clay ☐ papier-mâché ☐ wood ☐ other _____

to create a new type of bead. Give your new creation a name

and write ☐ _____ sentences ☐ _____

paragraphs about it.

☐ 10. Using a bag of mixed beads, make a bracelet or necklace for a friend.

☐ 11. Research the different types of beads using ☐ books ☐ the

Internet ☐ other _____. Write a ☐ sentence

☐ paragraph ☐ page about the different types of beads you like and tell why you chose those beads.

☐ 12. Pretend that you are a mathematician. Using a bag of mixed

beads, choose _____ different sizes of beads.

Compare the beads. Use a ruler to measure their size. Use your measurement findings to create math problems. What is the same and what is different about them? Report your findings to a ☐ friend ☐ teacher.

☐ 13. Pretend that you and _____ friends are on an

archaeological dig. During the excavation your team discovers an unknown bead. Your job is to prepare a statement telling the world where the bead was found, what it looks like, and what your team has decided to do with it. Prepare your statement, illustrate your bead, and tell a friend about it. Write ☐

_____ sentence(s) ☐ _____

paragraph(s) ☐ _____ page(s).

☐ 14. Choose a friend and make friendship bracelets for each other.

☐ 15. Choose a partner. Using a bag of mixed beads, see how many different patterns of beads you can make. Record your answer and compare with your partner's answer. Did you discover the same patterns? Who had more? Write down your patterns.

Copyright © 2008 by John Wiley & Sons, Inc.

**Art Activities**

# Beading and Jewelry
## Tasks *(continued)*

☐ 16. Create an ornament for the season of your choice. Be as creative as you would like.

Suggestions for supplies:

☐ *Spring:* fresh or dried flowers, leaves, ribbons, lace

☐ *Summer:* seashells, fake pearls, green leaves, little sea creatures made of clay

☐ *Fall:* autumn leaves, nutshells, horse chestnut seed shells

☐ *Winter:* pine needles, pinecones, cranberries, tiny red bells

☐ 17. Create a special folder in which to keep samples of beadwork, including drawings, magazine pictures, and copies from books or the Internet. This folder will allow you to save beading ideas that you may want to try.

Copyright © 2008 by John Wiley & Sons, Inc.

**Differentiated Instruction Made Easy**

# Chapter 10

# Music Activities

Musical task cards, task wheels, and contracts coordinate academics at any level with whatever the students know and will learn about music. The activities in this chapter are intended to interest everyone in different forms of tuneful and lyrical communication. Be sure to permit students to investigate whatever is pleasant to their own musical ears. This may mean that the teacher will need to purchase earplugs!

# Music Contract

I, _____, will play in this symphony of learning about music.

I will follow the conductor's direction for _____ tasks and choose

_____ that tune me in. I will work harmoniously and complete

this rhythmic adventure by _____.
                                    Date

_____
        Conductor

_____
        Musician

Copyright © 2008 by John Wiley & Sons. Inc.

# Music Tasks

☐   1. Pick an instrument and find a recording that demonstrates the sound of this instrument. Share your discovery ☐ with a friend ☐ with the class.

☐   2. Find ☐ kitchen items ☐ classroom items ☐ other _____ that can be used as musical instruments.

☐   3. Invent a musical instrument using materials of your choice.

☐   4. Write the words of your favorite song ☐ on paper ☐ on a whiteboard ☐ other _____ and share them with your friends. You may also sing the words and accompany yourself on a musical instrument.

☐   5. Make a musical ☐ scrapbook ☐ collage ☐ bulletin board.

☐   6. Pick out some music you like. Make up a dance to do ☐ alone ☐ with friends that uses ☐ only parts of your body ☐ every bone in your body.

☐   7. Compose a song to help ☐ you ☐ a friend learn ☐ math facts ☐ spelling words ☐ other _____.

☐   8. Listen to a song that ☐ has no words ☐ has words and create a ☐ drawing ☐ painting ☐ other _____ that shows how the music makes you feel.

☐   9. ☐ Write and sing ☐ Record and sing your own words to a song you like.

☐ 10. Invite _____ friends to a concert for which you have chosen the music. This can be a concert about ☐ any music ☐ music that creates a particular mood ☐ music that tells about another country ☐ music that represents a particular category. Make a program to hand out at your concert.

☐ 11. ☐ Write an essay about ☐ Record a speech about your musical preference.

☐ 12. Act out _____ song(s) or piece(s) of music ☐ alone ☐ with your friends. Pantomime the singer, the instruments, the movements, and so on.

☐ 13. Create a musical score using ☐ street sounds ☐ household sounds ☐ classroom sounds ☐ other _____. Record your music and listen to it ☐ alone ☐ with friends.

Copyright © 2008 by John Wiley & Sons, Inc.

# Music Tasks *(continued)*

☐ 14. Plan a parade. ☐ Pick the music and instruments. ☐ Design costumes.

☐ 15. Listen to music from another country and ☐ write ☐ record ☐ illustrate what you learn about that country's music, life, history, and so on.

☐ 16. Make a list of sounds that are musical to your ears, and another list of sounds that you consider just plain noise. Make a ☐ recording ☐ other _____ of these sounds.

☐ 17. Make up a song about ☐ your life ☐ an event ☐ a surprise ☐ other _____.

☐ 18. Think of _____ animal sounds. ☐ Alone ☐ With friends create a song using these sounds.

☐ 19. Make a drum. ☐ Create rhythm patterns. ☐ Record these sounds.

☐ 20. Make a dictionary of terms you must know to understand music. ☐ Write definitions. ☐ Illustrate each term.

☐ 21. ☐ Read a newspaper article ☐ Pick a fairy tale ☐ Watch a TV show and write a song about it. ☐ Record it. ☐ Sing it to your friends.

☐ 22. Pick a song. Listen to the words. ☐ Write ☐ Record ☐ Illustrate ☐ Act out the plot of the song. ☐ Make ☐ Wear a costume for this performance.

☐ 23. Interview people ☐ of differing ages ☐ from different countries ☐ of different cultures ☐ other _____ to discover their musical preferences. ☐ Chart your results. ☐ Summarize your results ☐ in writing ☐ on video.

☐ 24. Learn a song from a foreign country. Teach it to others who are interested in learning another language.

☐ 25. Listen to different recordings. ☐ Write ☐ Record ☐ Illustrate ☐ Act out how each one makes you feel.

☐ 26. Create a rhythm pattern.

☐ 27. Make a monthly calendar of musical events in your community. List performers, times, ticket prices, location, and other facts that interest you. ☐ Illustrate the calendar.

☐ 28. Design _____ music tasks of your own.

Copyright © 2008 by John Wiley & Sons. Inc.

# Instrument Task Wheels

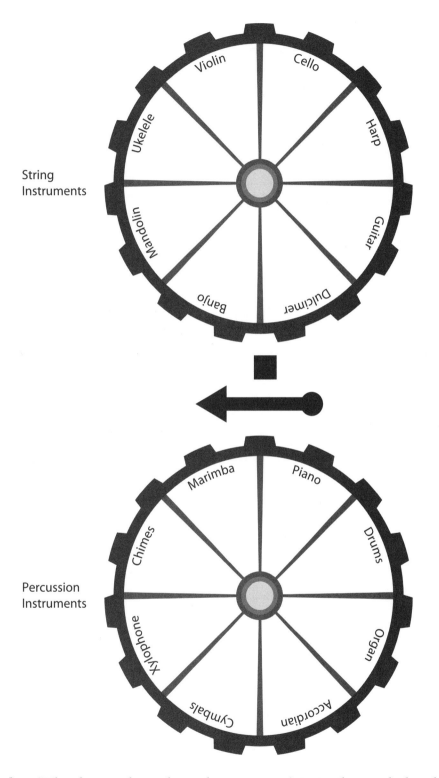

String Instruments

Percussion Instruments

*Note to teacher:* Wheels may be enlarged as appropriate to the grade level.

Copyright © 2008 by John Wiley & Sons, Inc.

# Instrument Task Wheels *(continued)*

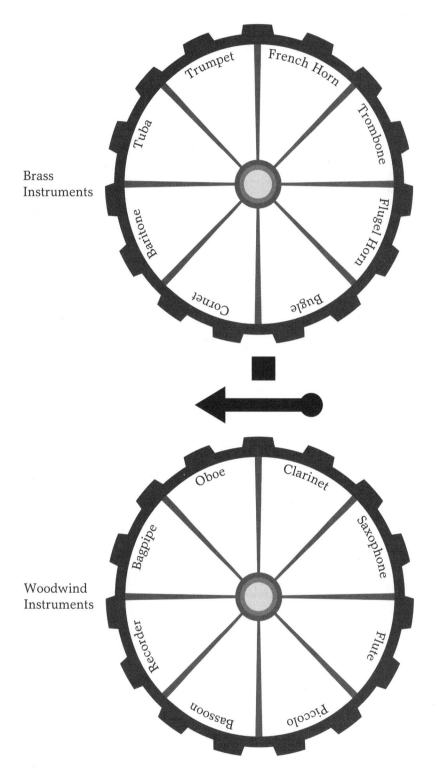

Brass Instruments

Woodwind Instruments

*Note to teacher:* Wheels may be enlarged as appropriate to the grade level.

**Differentiated Instruction Made Easy**

Copyright © 2008 by John Wiley & Sons, Inc.

# Instrument Task Cards

What family is this instrument in?

How do you know?

What kinds of music fit this instrument?

What is this instrument made of?

What is the history of this instrument?

Name _____ musicians who are famous for playing this musical instrument.

Enter into your musical encyclopedia all the information you can get about this musical instrument (pictures, drawings, facts, and so on).

☐ Write ☐ Draw ☐ Tape ☐ Act out how this instrument makes you feel.

Find _____ CDs that feature this instrument.

Act out playing this instrument.

Copyright © 2008 by John Wiley & Sons, Inc.

**Music Activities**

# Instrument Task Cards *(continued)*

Make up _____ tasks that will teach you more about this instrument.

Who invented this instrument and how was it invented?

Does this instrument need special care? If so, what kind?

Interview a musician who plays this instrument. See if this person will visit your class.

On what occasions (holidays, festivals, and so on) is this instrument featured?

To what key is this instrument tuned?

Would you like to have this instrument as a friend? Why? Why not?

Can you imitate the sound of this instrument?

Make instrument flash cards with name, family, and other important information on the back of the card. Test your knowledge.

Copyright © 2008 by John Wiley & Sons. Inc.

**Differentiated Instruction Made Easy**

# Type of Music
# Task Cards and Wheel

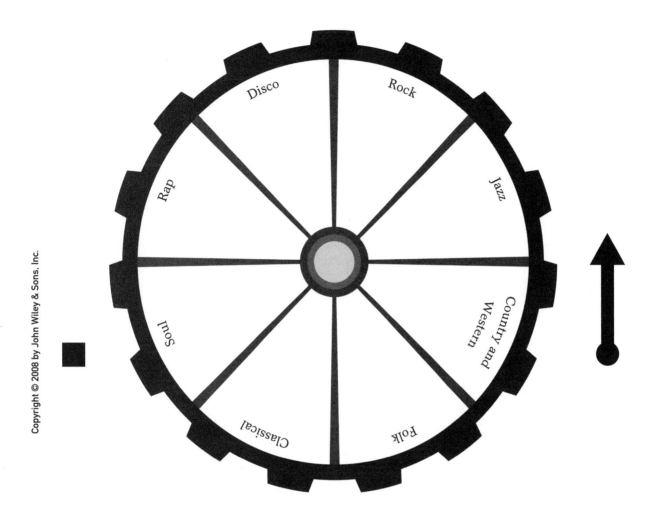

Copyright © 2008 by John Wiley & Sons, Inc.

*Note to teacher:* Wheels may be enlarged as appropriate to the grade level.

# Type of Music
# Task Cards and Wheel *(continued)*

Name _____ musicians who have made this musical form famous.

What local record stores sell this music?

Name _____ instruments that are commonly used with this form of music.

Where can you go in your community to hear this music?

Do a ☐ collage ☐ painting ☐ other _____ that describes how this music makes you feel.

Who do you think would like this music?

Copyright © 2008 by John Wiley & Sons. Inc.

**Differentiated Instruction Made Easy**

# Type of Music
# Task Cards and Wheel *(continued)*

Copyright © 2008 by John Wiley & Sons. Inc.

Get ☐ a CD ☐ sheet music of
_____ examples of this
music. Share your samples with the
class.

Would this music make someone feel
☐ happy ☐ sad ☐ angry ☐ confused
☐ annoyed? Why?

Where or how did this music
originate?

What local radio stations play this
music?

**Music Activities**

# Task Cards (Using Staff Paper)

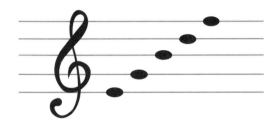

Copy the above example onto your staff paper and give the notes the right letters.

Clue: Every Good Boy Does Fine!

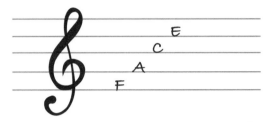

Look at this example and copy the notes in the right places on your staff paper. Play these notes on ☐ a piano ☐ other instrument.

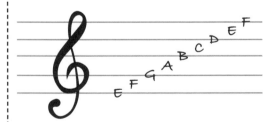

Copy the notes onto your staff paper. Circle the FACE notes and put little squares around the EGBDF notes (Every Good Boy Does Fine).

Pick out a line or phrase from sheet music. Copy it onto your staff paper. Play it on ☐ a piano ☐ other instrument.

*Note:* Staff paper is provided at the end of the chapter.

**Differentiated Instruction Made Easy**

Copyright © 2008 by John Wiley & Sons, Inc.

# Task Cards (Using Staff Paper)

## *(continued)*

Copyright © 2008 by John Wiley & Sons, Inc.

1 2 3 4 5 6 7 8 9 0
C D E F G A B C D E

Using the above code, the staff paper, and your phone number, write a short tune on staff paper. Play it on the □ xylophone □ piano □ harpsichord □ other _____. Now come up with other phone numbers such as the police station, the fire station, the home of your friend, your favorite pizza parlor, the super ice cream store, other _____, and compose more wonderful music. You may become famous!

Use these words in any order and write your own musical score on staff paper.

| Bag | Fad |
| Bad | Abe |
| Dad | Bee |
| Egg | Be |
| Cab | Beg |
| Fed | Ace |
| Bead | Face |
| Gab | |

Now think of other words that use the letters A, B, C, D, E, F, G and continue on. Oh, what beautiful music you can make!

1 2 3 4 5 6 7 8 9 0
C D E F G A B C D E

Write a song on staff paper using □ numbers □ letters instead of notes. Examples:

Put any notes on your staff paper. Then play them on the □ piano □ harpsichord □ xylophone □ other _____. (If you decide to get fancy, find a friend who can help you with showing measurement of time in music.)

**Music Activities**

# Music Wheel and Task Cards

| | |
|---|---|
| What is this symbol called? What does it mean? Where and how is it used?  | Make a flash card for this symbol, with the symbol on the front and its name on the back. Have your friends spin the wheel and make flash cards with their symbols. Test each other until you know all the symbols by name. |
| Copy some sheet music onto staff paper. Each time your symbol appears, circle it in a color according to the following code:<br><br>⬯— Red     ♫ Orange<br>♩ Yellow    # Brown<br>♪ Green     𝄞 Black<br>♩ Blue      𝄢 Pink<br>♬ Purple | Count and graph the number of times this symbol appears in two different pieces of sheet music. |
| What musical symbols can you discover from sheet music that are not on your wheel? Make your own wheel. | Use this symbol in making a drawing or cartoon or doodle.<br><br>Example: ____♩____ |

Copyright © 2008 by John Wiley & Sons. Inc.

**Differentiated Instruction Made Easy**

# Staff Paper

Copyright © 2008 by John Wiley & Sons. Inc.

# Chapter 11

# Imagine-Ifs: Fantasy Activities

If I were a yellow marigold . . . or a robot in the year 2210 . . . or lived all alone on a deserted island in the middle of an undiscovered ocean . . . or if I were a clown who could make the whole world happy . . . or . . . .

We live in a society of auditory and visual addicts. The dreamers, the creative thinkers, represent a small percentage of our population. But a faint inner voice insists that every human has the potential for creative output.

So another spaceship takes off for points unknown—and the TV announces a new cure for freckles. Join the "mission not so impossible" and follow the unknown path to the mysterious land of imagination.

Learners who make use of the materials in this chapter will participate in creative activities that remove the fear of wrong answers while enhancing creativity. The innovations offered involve imagination and fantasy, encompass all areas of the curriculum, and provide opportunities to use a variety of learning tools and approaches.

Multilevel spinners, task cards, and worksheets will entice all learners who dare to think creatively—and even the less daring learners will be hooked in no time at all.

Incorporate the style and format that best fits your learning environment. The activities in this chapter lend themselves readily to the learning center and group approaches.

Creativity seeds must be planted before they can grow. Although some learners will be ready to forge ahead, others will initially need group support and reinforcement. For many, this may be the first step down the path of lifelong creative adventure.

# Fantasy Suggestions

Here is a sample list of ideas. It is just a start!

| | |
|---|---|
| The president of _____ | A wave in the ocean |
| A very old person | A dinosaur |
| A fairy godmother | A tree |
| A movie star | A fish |
| A person who is blind | A shadow |
| A person in a wheelchair | A creature from another planet |
| A person who is deaf | A bird |
| A person with learning challenges | A magnificent flower |
| A very smart person | An old rocking chair |
| A person who has no friends | A sunrise |
| A witch | An animal |
| A robot | A shooting star |
| An inventor | A wonderful breeze |
| A computer | A sunset |

Copyright © 2008 by John Wiley & Sons, Inc.

# Imagine-If Cards

| | | |
|---|---|---|
| A witch | A treasure chest | A pot of gold at the end of a rainbow |
| A person in a wheelchair | A person flying in a hot air balloon | A grandma and grandpa in rocking chairs |
| A pot of flowers with faces, arms, and so on talking | A rat in a maze | A cat dressed up in hat and tails |
| A shaggy dog | A giraffe with a very long neck | A wishbone |
| A broken coffee mug | A car with a flat tire | A happy child |

Copyright © 2008 by John Wiley & Sons. Inc.

**Imagine-Ifs: Fantasy Activities**

# Imagine-If Cards *(continued)*

| | | |
|---|---|---|
| A sad child | A musical instrument with arms, face, legs that is dancing | A dancing snowman |
| An apple with a worm coming out of it | A fairy godmother | A spaceship |
| A covered wagon, drawn by horses | A teacher | An airplane |
| A king and queen | A snake | A court jester |
| A lion | An old house | A castle |

Copyright © 2008 by John Wiley & Sons. Inc.

**Differentiated Instruction Made Easy**

# Imagine-If Application

Copyright © 2008 by John Wiley & Sons, Inc.

I, _____, wish to pretend I am _____

from the fantasy paradise known as _____. I have chosen to

create _____.

I wish to "imagine if" from _____ to _____.
                                    Date                          Date

_____
Signature of Imagine-Ifer

_____
Signature of Reality Official

# Imaginations

☐ Write ☐ Record ☐ Illustrate ☐ Act out

☐ Other _____

☐ 1. What was easy?

☐ 2. What was difficult?

☐ 3. What made you ☐ happy ☐ sad ☐ excited ☐ angry ☐ bored
☐ confused ☐ scared ☐ joyful ☐ other _____,
and why?

☐ 4. Would you want to "imagine if" you were the same person or
thing again? Why or why not?

☐ 5. What did you learn about pretending?

Copyright © 2008 by John Wiley & Sons. Inc.

# Deserted Island

Copyright © 2008 by John Wiley & Sons. Inc.

You have just discovered paradise—a dream come true! It is fabulous. The birds sing all day. The ocean sounds like a symphony. Draw all the creatures and features you wish your paradise to have. Use the island shown here, or design your own. Then ☐ write ☐ tell ☐ make a poster ☐ make an audio recording ☐ make a video recording ☐ other information about:

☐ Animal life          ☐ Politics

☐ Plant life           ☐ Leisure activities

☐ Transportation       ☐ Products

☐ Money                ☐ Crops

☐ Inhabitants          ☐ Hobbies

☐ Weather              ☐ Clothing

☐ Government           ☐ Inventions

☐ Special attractions  ☐ Other _____

☐ Religions

# Imagine-If Contract

*Why? Why not?* Pretending is fun and I may learn a lot, so I will put my name in the slot: _____. I will complete _____ imagination tasks, and I will complete _____ others if I am asked. Wishes and dreams can hardly wait, so I will finish these by this date: _____.

_____
Dreamer

_____
Dream Facilitator

Copyright © 2008 by John Wiley & Sons. Inc.

# Imagine-If Tasks

☐ 1. ☐ Write ☐ Record ☐ Act out ☐ Illustrate ☐ Keep a diary
☐ Draw a poster ☐ Draw a cartoon ☐ Other _____

   ☐ A wish       ☐ A hope
   ☐ A dream     ☐ An unknown
   ☐ A fear       ☐ Other _____

☐ 2. You have free choice! Express the feeling of different natural elements:

   ☐ Water   ☐ Rain    ☐ Clouds   ☐ Ocean
   ☐ Snow    ☐ Wood   ☐ Paper    ☐ Hot
   ☐ Cold     ☐ Wet    ☐ Dry     ☐ Other _____

☐ 3. Pretend that you are half (½) _____ and half (½) _____. ☐ Write a story ☐ Illustrate ☐ Make a poster ☐ Act out ☐ Record ☐ Other _____ what it would be like.

☐ 4. Draw a picture of your fantasy pet. ☐ Write ☐ Record a story about this pet and its life.

☐ 5. Think of an animal. Imagine that this animal can talk. ☐ Write ☐ Record ☐ Illustrate what happens when you become pals with this animal.

☐ 6. Imagine that you are a machine that ☐ makes ice cream ☐ fixes broken hearts ☐ manufactures smiles ☐ paints rainbows ☐ bakes chocolate chip cookies ☐ manufactures freckles ☐ other _____. ☐ Write ☐ Record ☐ Illustrate ☐ Act out what this incredible machine is like inside and out.

☐ 7. You have just landed on the planet Earth. You are a space creature. Choose your favorite way to describe ☐ what you find ☐ how you feel ☐ what you see ☐ other _____.

☐ 8. When you feel _____, imagine how it would be to feel _____. ☐ Write ☐ Record ☐ Illustrate ☐ Act out these opposite feelings.

☐ 9. Take a walk in another pair of shoes of your choice: ☐ ballet slippers ☐ torn sneakers ☐ cowboy boots ☐ hiking shoes. Choose a way to describe your life in these shoes.

☐ 10. Imagine that you are a _____ in the middle of a ☐ snowstorm ☐ earthquake ☐ sunny day ☐ desert ☐ tornado ☐ stormy day at sea ☐ big city ☐ deserted island ☐ other _____.

**Imagine-Ifs: Fantasy Activities**              **157**

Copyright © 2008 by John Wiley & Sons. Inc.

# Imagine-If Tasks *(continued)*

☐ 11. Imagine that you are a genius and can invent a machine to do anything you wish. What would you invent? _____.
☐ Write ☐ Record ☐ Illustrate ☐ Create ☐ Other _____.

☐ 12. Imagine that you have won $_____ (Jackpot!).
☐ List ☐ Illustrate ☐ Make a Collage ☐ Other _____ of what you would do with it.

☐ 13. Draw your image of what this world would look like from
☐ The top of a mountain          ☐ The moon
☐ The bottom of the ocean      ☐ Other _____

☐ 14. You have just been given a magic key. What would you unlock? _____. Select a way to tell about it.

☐ 15. You have _____ wishes. What would you wish for? _____. ☐ Write ☐ Record
☐ Illustrate ☐ Other _____ and why.

☐ 16. You are king or queen of the universe. You have _____ chances to change the world. What would you do? Tell about your changes in any way you wish.

☐ 17. ☐ Write ☐ Record ☐ Illustrate a story that begins with "I dreamed I was a _____, but when I woke up, I discovered that _____."
What happens next?

☐ 18. Pretend you are president of your ☐ school ☐ class ☐ family ☐ club ☐ neighborhood ☐ other _____. ☐ Write ☐ Record ☐ Illustrate ☐ Other _____ what you would do.

☐ 19. Pretend you could make all the rules. ☐ Write ☐ Illustrate ☐ Record ☐ Other _____ what they would be.

☐ 20. You have just landed on _____. What is it like?

☐ 21. Pretend you are a professional athlete. What sport would you choose? _____. ☐ Write ☐ Record ☐ Illustrate ☐ Other _____ what life would be like for you.

☐ 22. Pretend you are a ☐ rock star ☐ actor. ☐ Write ☐ Record ☐ Illustrate ☐ Other _____ what life would be like for you.

Copyright © 2008 by John Wiley & Sons. Inc.

# Imagine-If Idea Cards

You are the captain of this ship. You are free to go any place in the world! Plan your adventure. Make a map that shows where you will stop. Plan your itinerary for _____ days _____ years.

☐ Write ☐ Tape ☐ the reasons for your stops ☐ your adventures ☐ your fears ☐ your problems ☐ your marvelous surprises ☐ other _____.

You are the queen or king of the planet _____.
It is your desire to make this the perfect planet. ☐ Write ☐ Tape ☐ Illustrate what you would do to make yourself and your subjects happy.

Copyright © 2008 by John Wiley & Sons, Inc.

**Imagine-Ifs: Fantasy Activities**

# Imagine-If Idea Cards *(continued)*

You are the only clown in the whole wide world who can fill everyone's heart with joy.

☐ Write
☐ Act out
☐ Tape
☐ Illustrate
your plan of action.

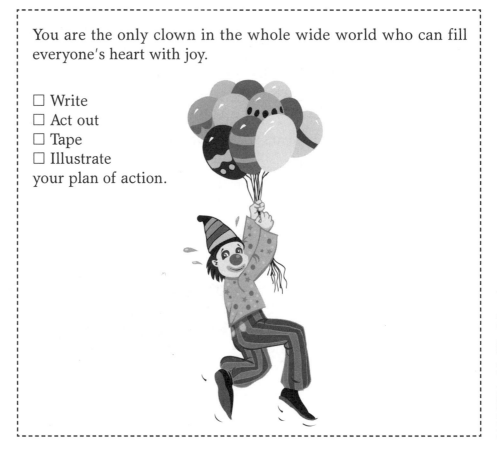

Copyright © 2008 by John Wiley & Sons, Inc.

**Differentiated Instruction Made Easy**

# Imagine-If Task Wheels

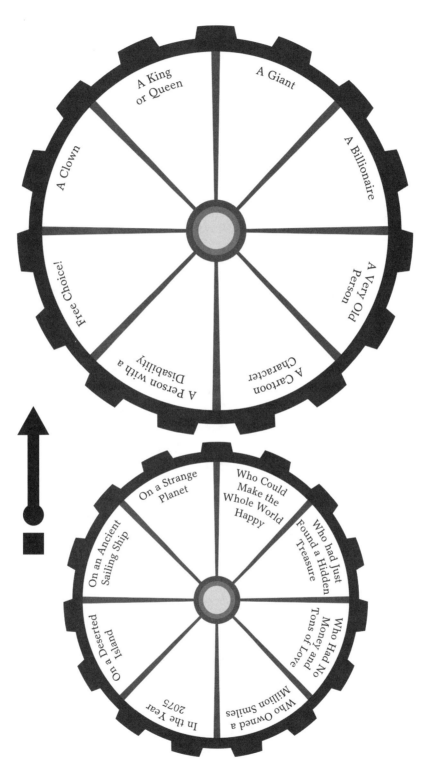

Copyright © 2008 by John Wiley & Sons, Inc.

*Note to teacher:* Wheels may be enlarged as appropriate to the grade level.

**Imagine-Ifs: Fantasy Activities**

**161**

# Imagine-If Task Wheels *(continued)*

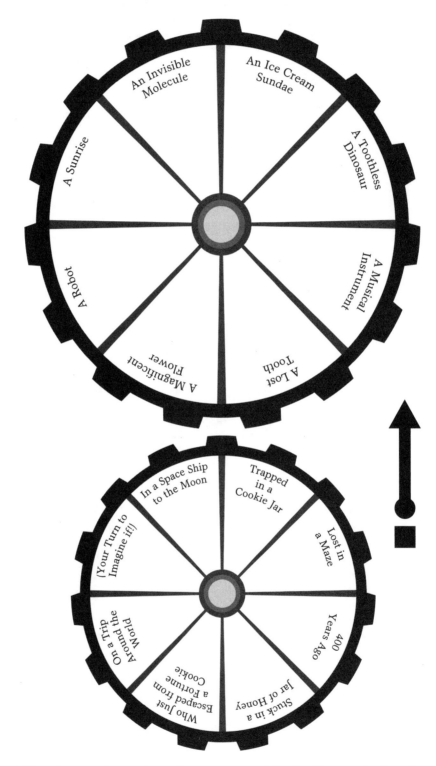

*Note to teacher:* Wheels may be enlarged as appropriate to the grade level.

Copyright © 2008 by John Wiley & Sons. Inc.

**Differentiated Instruction Made Easy**

# Imagine-If Task Cards for Use with Wheels

Copyright © 2008 by John Wiley & Sons, Inc.

Write about this Imagine-If.

Tell _____ friends about your Imagine-If.

Act it out with _____ friends.

Create ☐ a model ☐ a diorama ☐ a costume ☐ other _____ .

Write a play. Act it out with _____ others.

☐ Write ☐ Illustrate your own Imagine-If book.

Tape your own Imagine-If story.

Keep a diary of your Imagine-If adventures for _____ days.

Make a fantasy ☐ poster ☐ cartoon ☐ other _____ .

Do what you want to do—with permission, of course!

**Imagine-Ifs: Fantasy Activities**

# Chapter 12

# Peacemaking and Service Learning

It takes more than a multilevel miracle to create a positive atmosphere in any environment. It takes people working together—and teachers are people too! To make this happen, we need mutual cooperation, respect, and love.

Multilevel, multiuse, multi-effective sharing and caring activities can help because they are nonthreatening and can be used with students of any age who wish to participate. From the getting-to-know-you days of early September to the have-a-nice-summer days of June, there are many opportunities to encourage awareness of and sensitivity to the unique humanness of each and every one of us. We are special—you, and you, and you, and I. And our classrooms can reflect the ways we honor each one of us if we set them up to reinforce positive interactions and thereby extend heart-smart awareness into our communities.

This chapter includes contracts, task cards, wheels, and weekly diary sheets. For students who enjoy record keeping and graphing, a care-and-share chart is included. A multilevel gameboard (see Chapter 13) can be used to stimulate additional ideas.

The cards and wheels can be used to stimulate oral or written language. They can be used by one student, by learners working in pairs, or with groups to facilitate various kinds of interactions within a classroom. Many of these ideas can be extended into the school yard, cafeteria, or school bus. Additional ideas that are relevant to their worlds will come from the students themselves.

Duplicate the diary sheets so that each member of the class can keep a running record. Changes in group interactions and classroom attitudes will be much more noticeable if you can look back to where you all came from via individual diaries. Diaries are of course subjective while charts are objective measurements.

There are many ways to express one's thoughts and feelings and to grow and develop into a heart-smart caring and sharing human being. Including this aspect of curriculum development in our classrooms will result in a peaceful atmosphere conducive to learning.

# Peacemaker Contract

Copyright © 2008 by John Wiley & Sons, Inc.

I, _____, am a proud peacemaker. I am happy to take responsibility for my classroom, my community, my world (which is still quite small). I will do the following _____ tasks that I choose. I also agree to complete _____ tasks that my teacher chooses for me.

_____

Peacemaker

_____

Peace Facilitator

# Peacemaker Tasks

On a map (world, country, state, local, school, classroom, other) locate hot spots where peace is not the way of life. The students need to see and understand how much of the world is a hot spot and what "Let there be peace on Earth and let it begin with me" really means.

- ☐ 1. Design a ☐ button ☐ banner ☐ flag ☐ poster ☐ other _____ that illustrates peacemaking.

- ☐ 2. Mix colors—watercolors, computer colors—and describe how they make you feel. What would you like to do with the colors?

- ☐ 3. Using ☐ sand ☐ glitter ☐ stone ☐ fingerpaint ☐ other _____, make a list of textures and explain how they make you feel. Make a ☐ collage ☐ quilt ☐ diorama ☐ other _____.

- ☐ 4. Describe music you listen to ☐ to be peaceful ☐ to dance ☐ to do homework ☐ other _____.

- ☐ 5. Listen to the words of a song. List the number of feeling words you hear. Graph the number of negative words and the number of positive words. Look at your graph and decide if the song supports peacemaking.

- ☐ 6. With _____ friends record and graph the words you hear ☐ on the playground ☐ at lunch ☐ in a classroom ☐ on the bus ☐ while waiting in line ☐ other _____ that ☐ heal ☐ hurt.

- ☐ 7. With _____ classmates record and graph the words you hear or read that ☐ heal ☐ hurt ☐ on the television ☐ in a movie ☐ on the radio ☐ in the newspaper ☐ in a song ☐ other _____.

- ☐ 8. Write a letter of ☐ support for ☐ protest about _____ situations you wish to change. With teacher approval, send it to someone who can benefit from the information.

- ☐ 9. Make a ☐ book ☐ rap ☐ poem ☐ about you ☐ a friend named _____ ☐ a hero named _____ being a peacemaker.

- ☐ 10. Make a ☐ book ☐ rap ☐ poem about the _____ things that make this world "perfect" for you.

- ☐ 11. Design ☐ a poster ☐ comic strip ☐ other _____ of the things that are most ☐ enjoyable ☐ difficult ☐ confusing for you.

Copyright © 2008 by John Wiley & Sons. Inc.

# Peacemaker Tasks *(continued)*

☐ 12. Look up organizations ☐ on the Internet ☐ in library resources ☐ other _____ that are dedicated to bringing peace to our planet. Learn about them and share your information ☐ in a speech ☐ in an essay ☐ on a poster ☐ other _____.

☐ 13. Think about how you can support an organization that does the kind of things you believe in. Find out how they ☐ share information ☐ raise money, and organize a plan with _____ friends to share what you know.

☐ 14. With _____ friends write a script about a situation that hurts or heals and how you are able to solve the conflict. Act it out in ☐ your group ☐ your classroom ☐ other _____.

☐ 15. Draw ☐ a body ☐ a heart ☐ a hand. Inside your drawing ☐ write ☐ collage ☐ illustrate actions and words you want to keep in your life, and actions and words you want out of your life.

☐ 16. Sounds can hurt or heal. With friends, list various sounds and describe how they make you feel; for example, sirens, loud bangs, the ocean, and so on.

☐ 17. Make a peaceful concert with _____ friends using ☐ instruments you know how to play ☐ instruments you create ☐ your voices ☐ other _____.

☐ 18. Select one of the following statements: ☐ Sticks and stones can break my bones but names will never hurt me. ☐ Treat others the way you want to be treated. ☐ That's the way the cookie crumbles. ☐ Actions speak louder than words. ☐ Write ☐ Illustrate ☐ Create a ☐ poster ☐ collage ☐ diorama ☐ other _____ about how that statement makes you feel.

☐ 19. Select words you hear or use often such as *whatever*, *dude*, *sweet*, *cool*, or *awesome*. Create task cards with these words. Use the task cards to ☐ design a card game ☐ play with a gameboard ☐ play charades ☐ other _____.

☐ 20. Design a game with a board and spinner that teaches others about a way to create a peaceful planet or classroom.

☐ 21. Design a classroom mailbox that takes only positive messages. Be sure that all students in the class are included.

☐ 22. Using fabric paint, design and create a T-shirt that tells the world that you are a peacemaker.

Copyright © 2008 by John Wiley & Sons, Inc.

# Peacemaker Tasks *(continued)*

☐ 23. Share positive messages that start with ☐ I am ☐ I want for the classroom ☐ I hope for the world ☐ Other _____.

☐ 24. ☐ Design your own cartoon strips. ☐ Create a strip illustrating a conflict. ☐ Show what would change the conflict if what happened ☐ before ☐ during ☐ after had been different.

☐ 25. Organize a group of students to design ☐ an Olympics event ☐ a talent show ☐ a field day with ☐ rules ☐ games ☐ actions ☐ other _____ that will make your school a peace zone. Speak to your teacher, parents, and administrators and try to make peace a reality.

☐ 26. With _____ members of your class ☐ write commitments ☐ take actions ☐ adopt attitudes that can bring a positive climate to your classroom and make it a peace zone. Spread the word and share your ideas and actions with other classrooms.

☐ 27. How does the Bill of Rights help us live more peacefully? Select _____ articles from the Bill of Rights. Create a way to teach the meaning of the articles to others.

☐ 28. How does the Constitution help us live together more peacefully? Select _____ ideas from the Constitution and create your own special way to teach the concepts to others.

☐ 29. Imagine you are a ☐ new student ☐ student who does not speak English ☐ student who is just returning to school after the death of a family member ☐ other _____. Using a wheel or task cards, ☐ make a game ☐ make a collage ☐ role-play ☐ other activities that demonstrate how to make the student feel welcome.

☐ 30. You are a ☐ video game ☐ TV show ☐ movie ☐ music video critic. Develop a rating system that supports positive choices. Write reviews using your ratings and share them with ☐ friends ☐ your class.

☐ 31. You are the editor of a classroom newspaper that reports only positive and peaceful actions and attitudes. Using ☐ the computer ☐ classroom supplies ☐ other _____ create a ☐ weekly ☐ monthly paper.

☐ 32. You are a radio or TV talk show host who has conversations only about peaceful actions and attitudes. ☐ Plan ☐ Record ☐ Write a script for ☐ Act out a sample episode.

Copyright © 2008 by John Wiley & Sons, Inc.

**Differentiated Instruction Made Easy**

# Peacemaker Tasks *(continued)*

☐ 33. Many children's books in your school or community library deal with conflict resolution and peaceful actions. Pick out a book and read it. ☐ Write a report ☐ Share the book with another group of students ☐ Design a poster ☐ Interview the author ☐ Other _____.

☐ 34. Make a dictionary that defines words such as *cooperation, sharing, asking, empathy, violence,* and so on. Illustrate the dictionary using ☐ posters ☐ Web sites ☐ other _____.

☐ 35. Volunteer _____ hours a month ☐ in your school ☐ in your neighborhood ☐ in your community ☐ for an organization in a distant land. Record your time and actions.

☐ 36. Create and illustrate posters that complete the following phrases: ☐ Help is _____. ☐ Hope is _____. ☐ Caring is _____. ☐ Conflict is _____. ☐ Other _____.

☐ 37. On a computer, design or create a greeting card for a person ☐ who will be celebrating a special day ☐ who is sick ☐ who has lost a loved one ☐ with whom you've had a misunderstanding ☐ other _____.

☐ 38. Who is your hero in the ☐ classroom ☐ community ☐ world? ☐ Interview the person or ☐ Watch a TV show or video about him or her and share the information you have gathered with your ☐ class ☐ friends ☐ family.

☐ 39. Write lesson plans to teach ☐ younger kids ☐ older people ☐ other _____ to ☐ love ☐ care ☐ volunteer.

Copyright © 2008 by John Wiley & Sons, Inc.

# Sharing and Caring Wheel

*Note to teacher:* Wheels may be enlarged as appropriate to the grade level.

Copyright © 2008 by John Wiley & Sons. Inc.

**Differentiated Instruction Made Easy**

# Sharing and Caring Task Cards

| | |
|---|---|
| Write a story about this person. | Draw a picture of this person. |
| _____ a picture to give to this person. | Write a _____ to (for) this person. |
| Interview this person. Find out all you can in _____ minutes. Share what you have learned with _____. | Have this person interview you for _____ minutes. Share the interview with _____. |
| Do something nice for this person. Do not tell anyone. | Find out _____ of this person's favorite _____. |
| Talk to this person and find out _____ things you both like to do. List them ☐ on the board ☐ on a piece of paper ☐ in your diary. | What are this person's favorite<br>☐ TV shows?  ☐ Flowers?<br>☐ Foods?  ☐ Movie stars?<br>☐ Colors?  ☐ Things to do?<br>☐ Places?  ☐ Singers?<br>☐ Animals?  ☐ Web sites? |
| ☐ Write ☐ Record this person's biography ☐ alone ☐ with their help. | Make a timeline of the important events in this person's life. |

Copyright © 2008 by John Wiley & Sons, Inc.

# Sharing and Caring
## Task Cards *(continued)*

| | |
|---|---|
| Make a ☐ poster ☐ radio ad ☐ award advertising this person.  | Do something special for this person. See if he or she can guess what it was.  |
| What makes this person: ☐ feel good? ☐ feel bad?  | Do-your-own-thing card  |

Copyright © 2008 by John Wiley & Sons, Inc.

**Differentiated Instruction Made Easy**

# Feelie Wheelies

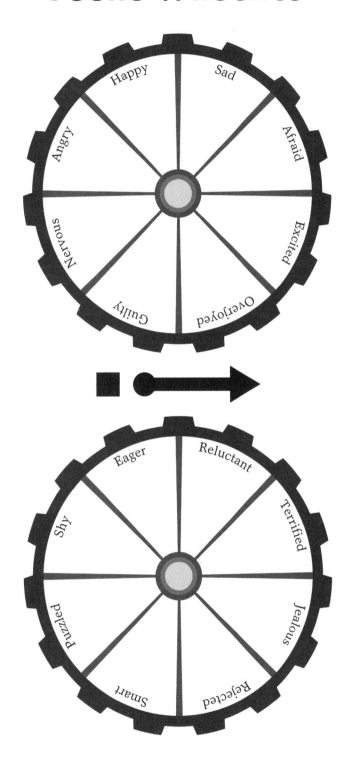

*Note to teacher:* Wheels may be enlarged as appropriate to the grade level.

Copyright © 2008 by John Wiley & Sons. Inc.

**Peacemaking and Service Learning**

# Feelie Wheelies Task Cards

| | |
|---|---|
| How would you help someone who is _____? | What could you make for someone who is _____ ? |
| What can you say to someone who is _____ ? | How can you relate to someone who is _____? |
| What would you do if someone made you feel _____? | How would you react if someone made you feel _____? |
| What makes you feel _____? | What makes the teacher _____? |
| What makes □ mother □ father □ family □ sister □ brother □ neighbor □ friend □ dog □ cat _____? | Who makes you feel _____? |
| When do you feel _____? | Why do you feel _____ ? |
| Where do you like to go when you feel _____? | Whom do you like to be with when you feel _____? |
| Count how many times today you felt _____. | How many times today did you make _____ feel _____? |

Copyright © 2008 by John Wiley & Sons. Inc.

**Differentiated Instruction Made Easy**

# Facing Feelings Worksheet

Choose a Facing Feelings task card. Then select a task.

Copyright © 2008 by John Wiley & Sons. Inc.

# Facing Feelings Tasks

☐ 1. ☐ Write ☐ Record how each person is feeling.

☐ 2. Make up a story that tells why you think these people are feeling the way they are.

☐ 3. Have you ever been in a situation like this? ☐ Write ☐ Record ☐ Orally relate a description of it.

☐ 4. Pretend that one person is you and the other person is your best friend. What is happening?

☐ 5. Pretend that one person is you and the other person is your ☐ sister ☐ brother ☐ mother ☐ father. What is happening?

☐ 6. Pretend that these people are your parents. What is happening?

☐ 7. Pretend that one of these people is your teacher and the other one is your mother. What is happening?

☐ 8. Pretend that you are one of the people and the other one is someone you don't like. What is happening?

☐ 9. One person is _____. The other person is _____. How did you contribute to how they are feeling?

☐ 10. ☐ Write ☐ Record a skit with _____ about what is happening. Make the characters anyone you choose.

☐ 11. _____ a picture that puts these two people in a scene that tells what made them feel that way.

☐ 12. Should you do anything to change the feeling of the people?

☐ 13. Is there anything you can do to help?

☐ 14. Have you ever felt both of these ways at the same time? ☐ Write ☐ Record about it.

☐ 15. Would you like to be in this situation? Which person would you choose to be?

☐ 16. If you were in this situation, which person would you *not* want to be?

Copyright © 2008 by John Wiley & Sons, Inc.

# Facing Feelings Task Cards

| | | | | | |
|---|---|---|---|---|---|
| Sad |  | Nervous | Angry |  | Happy |
| Terrified |  | Guilty | Happy |  | Happy |
| Angry |  | Angry | Smart |  | Shy |
| Eager |  | Reluctant | Eager |  | Eager |
| Reluctant | 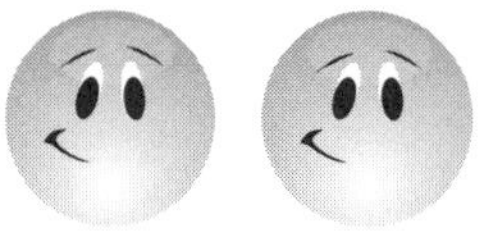 | Reluctant | Frightened |  | Nervous |
| Excited |  | Rejected | Happy |  | Shy |
| Nervous |  | Angry | Happy |  | Nervous |
| Overjoyed |  | Jealous | Guilty | 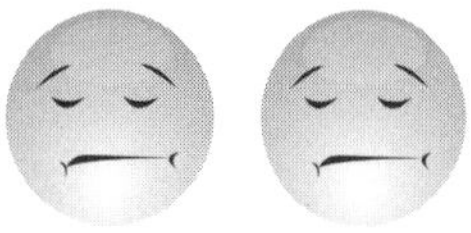 | Guilty |

Copyright © 2008 by John Wiley & Sons, Inc.

# Care and Share Chart

*And love in your heart wasn't put there to stay—love isn't love till you give it away.*
—Oscar Hammerstein II

Here are some special activities I do for others:

Name _____    Week of _____

| Activity | Mon. | Tues. | Wed. | Thur. | Fri. |
| --- | --- | --- | --- | --- | --- |

Copyright © 2008 by John Wiley & Sons, Inc.

# Weekly Journal Record

Week of _____

Dear Journal:

This week was ☐ fantastic ☐ awful ☐ pretty good ☐ so-so ☐ boring ☐ sad ☐ happy ☐ other _____ because:

_____

_____

_____

_____

_____

_____

Here's what my week looked like!

_____

_____

_____

_____

_____

_____

_____

_____

Copyright © 2008 by John Wiley & Sons, Inc.

# Part 2

# Gameboards, Wheels, Open-Ended Add-ons, and Awards

# Chapter 13

# Multilevel Gameboards

In this electronically driven, technical age there is still a place for games that are commercial, as well as for teacher-made games, in our classrooms. This chapter provides games that are student- and teacher-created and that give students opportunities to learn and reinforce academics as well as the life skills that are a vital part of true education. Open-ended gameboard samples are provided on the following pages. Supplemented with game pieces such as dice, markers in unique shapes, spinners, and other additions, these gameboards will add to the enjoyment of learning.

Multilevel gameboards are designed to

- Teach students the basics of game playing, such as sharing, taking turns, brainstorming—and, of course, patience
- Give students opportunities to participate in creative decision making
- Eliminate complicated instructions that often create negative interactions
- Permit students who function at different academic levels to interact around the rules of a game they created
- Release the teacher from the complicated task of acting as a referee
- Encourage the artistic abilities of each child who designs a gameboard and its vital components
- Positively reinforce students for their appropriate behaviors—and much more!

When using multilevel gameboards:

- Discuss the basic game rules with your learners. Teach them about games in which each player can be a winner. Discuss related aspects of decision making, sharing, and taking turns.
- The game rules must be established and understood by all players. Self-checking flash cards, peer and cross-age tutors, and actual task assignments can serve as stimuli for the moves, spins, dice rolling—whatever the players decide.
- Reinforce the students for appropriate game interactions and positive sharing as well as for task experiences. Encourage students to invent, design, and create new games, even if the skill level remains unchanged.

Add a center to your room where the supplies for game playing and creating are available. You will be amazed by their level of interest and cooperation when you give students the opportunity to learn in different ways and to enhance their academic and life skills.

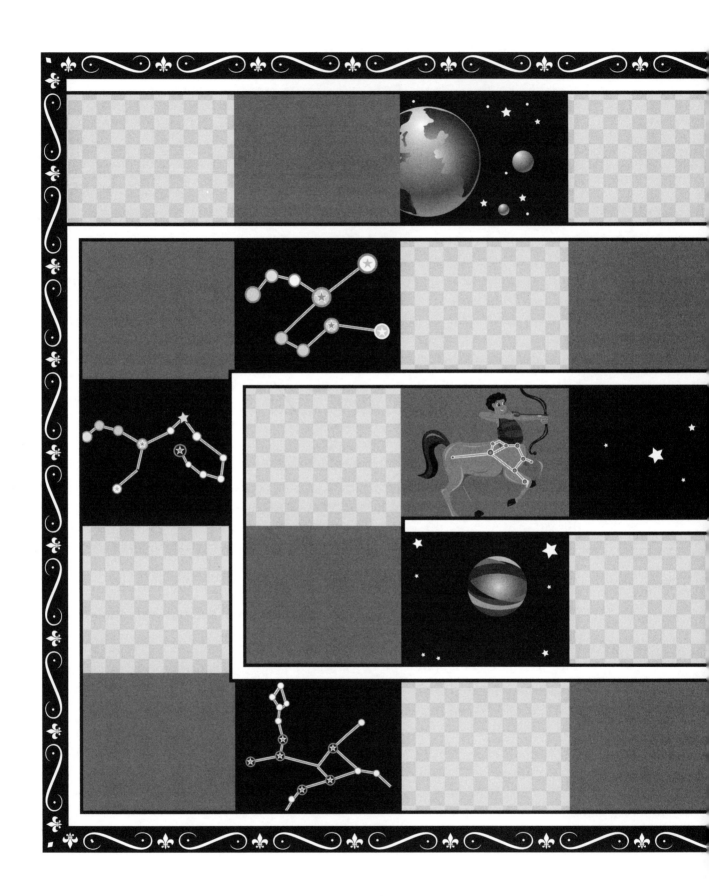

**Differentiated Instruction Made Easy**

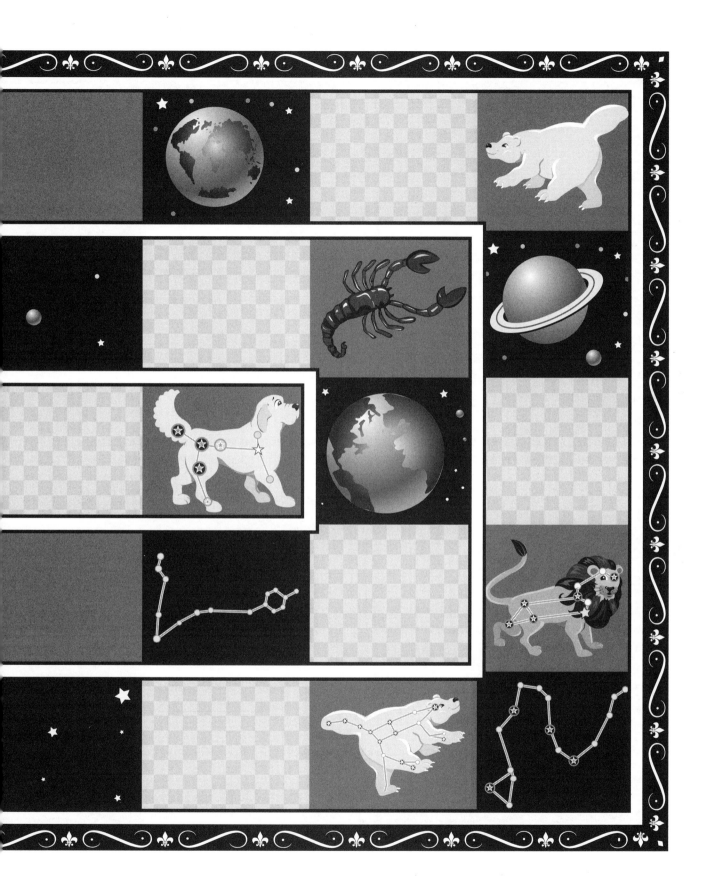

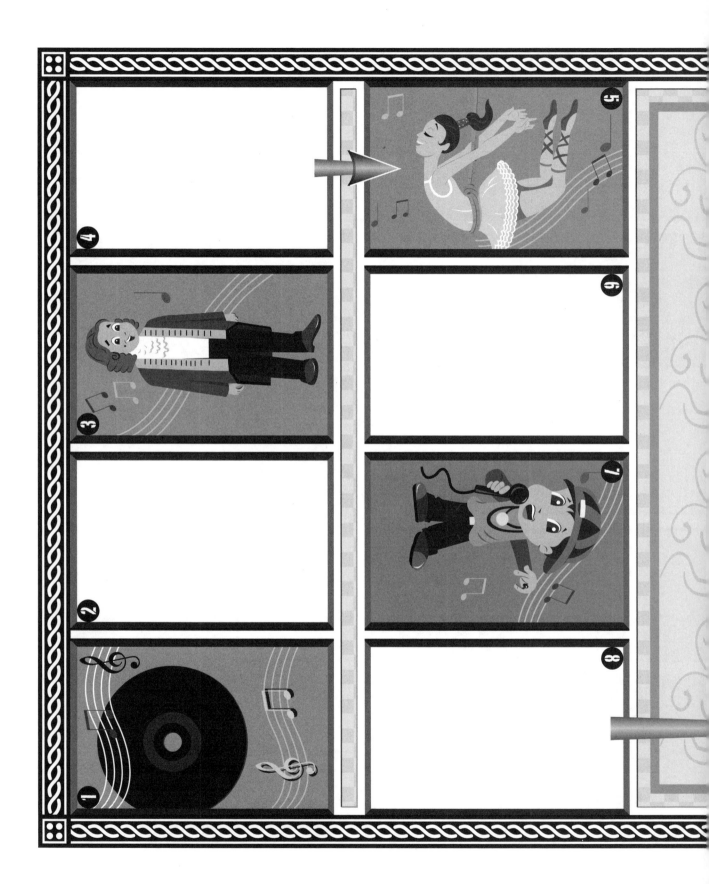

**Differentiated Instruction Made Easy**

**Differentiated Instruction Made Easy**

**Multilevel Gameboards**

**Differentiated Instruction Made Easy**

**Plug 'n' Play**
Plug the 'correct-plug' to poweron the computer!

**Multilevel Gameboards**

# Chapter 14

# Multilevel Task Wheels

Blank wheels of various sizes that may be combined to construct additional games are provided in this chapter. These wheels can also be used as stand-alone learning tools. Curriculum-specific wheels that are designed to teach specific skills appear throughout the book. The blank wheels provided here may be used for all curricular areas. Once the students become aware of their abilities to create learning tools, there is no end to their discovery and reinforcement of concepts that are new or challenging.

To create the wheels, you will need the following supplies:

- Tagboard
- Washers
- Brads
- Arrows (student-made or commercial)

There are three basic wheel designs. Each requires simple assembly and a splash of color. You may duplicate these basic designs for use with any of the task wheel ideas described in this book.

*Wheel 1:* This is the largest wheel. You may make as many divisions as you wish.

*Wheel 2:* This wheel is smaller than wheel 1. It can be used alone or placed on top of the larger wheel for a more complicated design that offers additional combinations for the learner.

*Wheel 3:* This is the smallest wheel. It can be used alone or on top of wheels 1 or 2 or both for increasingly complicated tasks. Students with more skills may prefer the three-wheel design, while less-skilled students may be more successful with a single wheel.

Page 86 provides an example of how three wheels can be used together.

# Wheels Used with Task Cards

Some chapters contain suggestions for wheels to be used with task cards. The student spins the wheel, takes a task card that goes with that wheel, and completes the task. For example, the arrow illustrated here is pointing at a triangle. The task card selected may say, "Name three objects that have this shape"; or the triangle (and each of the other shapes) could be assigned a numerical value, and a math task card could read, "Multiply this number by 4."

# Wheels Used by Themselves

Some chapters offer activities using wheels by themselves. In these cases, students simply answer the question or perform the task indicated by the spinner. The following example illustrates a double wheel with a spinner. The player would spin the smaller wheel and spinner, then describe the object toward which the spinner points (such as "Name something orange you can taste").

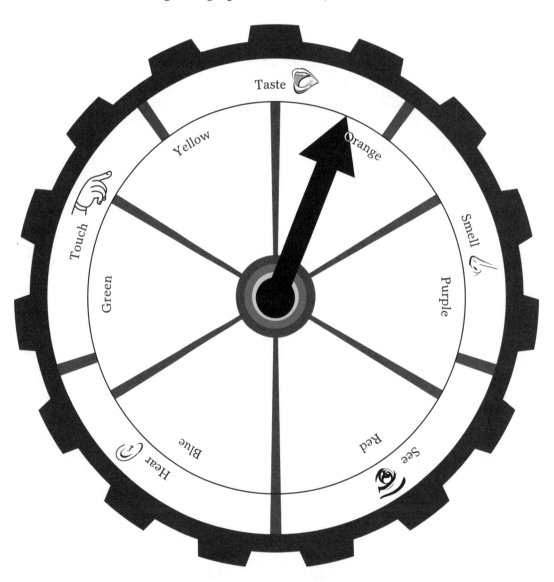

# Chapter 15

# Open-Ended Add-ons

- Journal sheet
- Staff paper
- Graph paper
- Cartoon strips
- Game instruction form
- Open-ended contract (for more bright ideas!)
- Calendar

# Journal Sheet

Name _____

Day of the Week _____ Date _____

Dear Journal: _____

_____

_____

_____

_____

_____

_____

_____

How I feel today:

_____

_____

_____

_____

_____

_____

_____

_____

Copyright © 2008 by John Wiley & Sons, Inc.

**Differentiated Instruction Made Easy**

# Staff Paper

Copyright © 2008 by John Wiley & Sons, Inc.

# Graph Paper

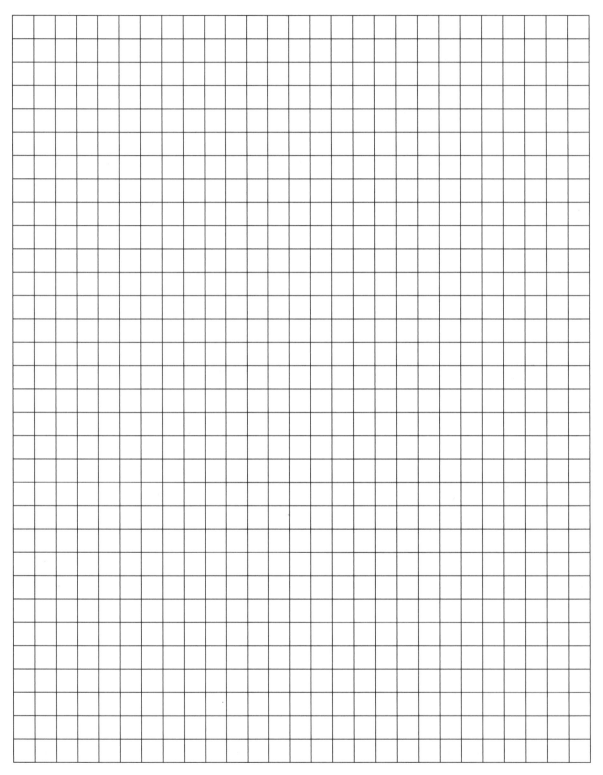

Copyright © 2008 by John Wiley & Sons. Inc.

# Cartoon Strips

Copyright © 2008 by John Wiley & Sons. Inc.

**Open-Ended Add-ons**

# Game Instruction Form

Title of game: _____

Number of persons who can play: _____ Ages: _____

Inventor(s): _____

_____

Game Description: _____

_____

_____

_____

Rules: _____

1. _____

2. _____

3. _____

4. _____

5. _____

6. _____

7. _____

8. _____

9. _____

10. _____

Materials Needed: _____

_____

Other: _____

_____

_____

_____

Copyright © 2008 by John Wiley & Sons, Inc.

# Open-Ended Contract

I, _____ ,

Copyright © 2008 by John Wiley & Sons, Inc.

_____
Signature

_____
Signature

# Calendar

| Sun | Mon | Tue | Wed | Thu | Fri | Sat |
|-----|-----|-----|-----|-----|-----|-----|
|     |     |     |     |     |     |     |
|     |     |     |     |     |     |     |
|     |     |     |     |     |     |     |
|     |     |     |     |     |     |     |
|     |     |     |     |     |     |     |
|     |     |     |     |     |     |     |

Copyright © 2008 by John Wiley & Sons. Inc.

**Differentiated Instruction Made Easy**

# Chapter 16

# Awards

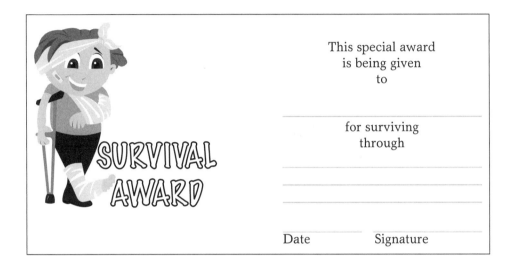

This special award
is being given
to

_____

for surviving
through

Date            Signature

# Awards

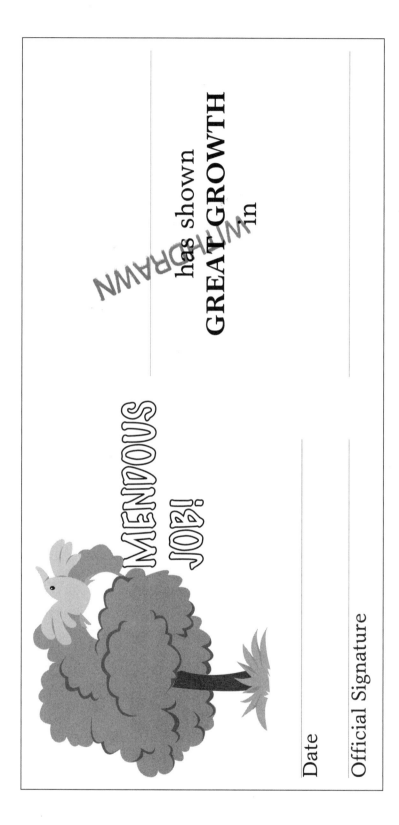

**TREE-MENDOUS JOB!**

has shown
**GREAT GROWTH** in

WITHDRAWN

Date _____

Official Signature _____

Copyright © 2008 by John Wiley & Sons, Inc.

# Awards *(continued)*

Copyright © 2008 by John Wiley & Sons. Inc.

EGG STRA SPECIAL AWARD

To _____

in recognition of a
tough task well
done in the area of

_____

on this day

_____

(long to be remembered)

Head Chicken Signature _____

# Awards *(continued)*

has made
great strides
in

Date

Timer

A FINE FINISH!

Copyright © 2008 by John Wiley & Sons. Inc.